P9-DWK-637

THE BOOK OF
APPETIZERS

THE BOOK OF
APPETIZERS

JUNE BUDGEN

Photography by
PER ERICSON

HPBooks®

ANOTHER BEST SELLING VOLUME FROM HPBooks

Published by HPBooks, a division of Price Stern Sloan, Inc.
360 N. La Cienega Blvd., Los Angeles, CA 90048
ISBN: 0-89586-482-7
Library of Congress Card Number: 86-81044
9 8 7 6 5 4 3

By arrangement with Salamander Books Ltd. and Merehurst Press,
London.

NOTICE: The information contained in this book is true and complete to
the best of our knowledge. All recommendations are made without any
guarantees on the part of the author or Price Stern Sloan. The author and
publisher disclaim all liability in connection with the use of this
information.

© Merehurst Limited and June Budgen 1986
All rights reserved. No part of this publication may be reproduced,
stored in a retrieval system, or transmitted, in any form or by any means
without the prior permission in writing of the publisher, nor be
otherwise circulated in any form of binding or cover other than that in
which it is published and without a similar condition including this
condition being imposed on the subsequent purchaser.

Editors: Rebecca La Brum, Susan Tomnay, Beverly Le Blanc, Chris Fayers
Designers: Susan Kinealy, Roger Daniels, Richard Slater, Stuart Willard
Food stylist: June Budgen
Photographer: Per Ericson
Typeset by Lineage
Color separation by Fotographics Ltd., London-Hong Kong
Printed in Belgium by Proost International Book Production

CONTENTS

INTRODUCTION

It is customary to serve appetizers as a start to a luncheon or dinner, but they can also be combined to make a varied and interesting complete meal.

For a formal dinner, choose an appetizer that is light but piquant so it will enhance the meal that is to follow. When an appetizer is served before a salad or a light main course, a more substantial dish, such as an individual quiche, would be more appropriate.

Appetizers for a cocktail party should be "finger food" that can be picked up and eaten with one hand. These parties require a great deal of preparation and I suggest choosing some of the dishes that can be cooked ahead of time and frozen, ready to reheat just before serving. Some appetizers which freeze well are small quiches, meatballs, pizzas, yeast rolls and filo pastries. Don't forget – if some of the finger food is a bit messy to eat, provide lots of small napkins.

You don't have to be a blue ribbon chef to produce a spectacular meal consisting of all appetizers, and a meal like this is especially suited to picnics where guests nibble all day. I am not allowed to appear at picnics without my Egg and Caviar Spread, page 91, and yet, like most of the recipes in this book, it is very easy to make.

SPICY FISH BALLS

1 lb. white-fish fillets
1 teaspoon grated fresh gingerroot
1 teaspoon salt
4 green onions, finely chopped
1½ teaspoons curry powder
3 eggs
1 cup fine dry bread crumbs
3 tablespoons sesame seeds
Vegetable oil for deep-frying
Lemon slices
Plain yogurt, if desired

In a fish poacher or large saucepan, poach fish in simmering water. Flake fish, discarding any skin and bones.

Place fish in a bowl and stir in gingerroot, salt, green onions and curry powder. Beat 1 egg; add to fish mixture and blend well. Shape mixture into 24 equal balls.

In a shallow dish, beat remaining 2 eggs. On a sheet of wax paper, mix bread crumbs and sesame seeds. Dip fish balls in egg, then roll in crumb mixture to coat. In a deep, heavy saucepan, heat about 2 inches of oil to 375F (190C) or until a 1-inch bread cube turns golden brown in about 50 seconds. Add fish balls, a few at a time, and cook until golden on all sides. Drain on paper towels. Serve hot or warm with lemon slices. If desired, offer yogurt for dipping. Makes 24.

- SEAFOOD COCKTAIL SAUCE -

Assorted seafood, such as cooked jumbo
   shrimps, oysters on-the-half-shell and
   Pickled Squid (page 34)
1¼ cups whipping cream
2 teaspoons prepared horseradish
1 tablespoon tomato sauce
2 tablespoons tomato paste
Few drops of hot-pepper sauce
Squeeze of lemon juice
Salt and black pepper to taste

Shell and devein each cooked jumbo
shrimp. Cover with plastic wrap and
refrigerate until ready to serve. Cover
and refrigerate other seafood.

In a bowl, stir together cream,
horseradish, tomato sauce, tomato
paste and hot-pepper sauce. Stir in
lemon juice, salt and black pepper.

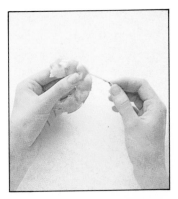

For a stiffer consistency, beat the
mixture until slightly thickened but
still thin enough to drop freely from a
spoon. Cover and refrigerate up to 3
days. To serve, place bowl of sauce in
center of a platter. Arrange shelled,
deveined shrimp and other seafood of
your choice around sauce. Serve
immediately. Makes about 1½ cups.

SEAFOOD PÂTÉ

1 lb. white-fish fillets
6 tablespoons butter
6 green onions, chopped
1 garlic clove, crushed
1 lb. uncooked shrimp, shelled, deveined
½ lb. scallops, if desired
2 tablespoons cognac or brandy
½ cup whipping cream
1 tablespoon lemon juice
1 teaspoon paprika
About ⅛ teaspooon red (cayenne) pepper
Salt to taste

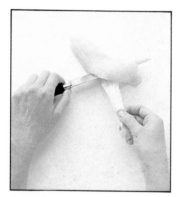

Remove any skin from fish. Pull out any bones, then cut in chunks and set aside.

Melt butter in a large skillet over medium-low heat. Add green onions and cook, stirring, 2 minutes. Stir in garlic, fish, uncooked shrimp and scallops, if desired. Cook, stirring often, until shrimp turn pink and fish flakes. Remove from heat. Warm cognac or brandy in a small saucepan. Ignite, pour over fish mixture and let flames die down.

Stir in cream, lemon juice, paprika and red pepper. Pour cooled seafood mixture into a food processor fitted with a metal blade. Process until smooth. Season with salt. Pour mixture into 1 large or several small serving dishes, cover and refrigerate until firm. Decorate with lemon slices, dill sprigs and cooked small shrimp, if desired. Serve with crackers, melba toast or celery sticks; provide a knife for spreading. Serves 8 to 10.

SEAFOOD TOASTS

12 slices firm-textured white bread
½ lb. skinned white-fish fillets
½ lb. uncooked shrimp, shelled, deveined
2 eggs
1 tablespoon dry sherry or ginger wine
¼ teaspoon shredded fresh gingerroot
1 tablespoon soy sauce
½ teaspoon salt
1 tablespoon cornstarch
Italian parsley sprigs, if desired
Vegetable oil for deep-frying

Cut a 2¾-inch square from center of each bread slice. Cut each square diagonally in half.

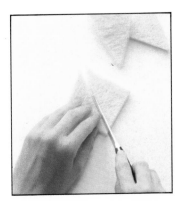

Cut fish in chunks. Place fish, shrimp, 1 egg, sherry, gingerroot, soy sauce, salt and cornstarch in a food processor fitted with a metal blade. Process to make a smooth paste. Spread seafood paste evenly over bread triangles.

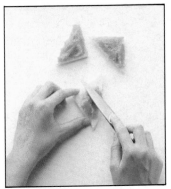

Beat remaining egg; brush over seafood-topped bread. Press a parsley sprig atop each bread triangle, if desired. In a deep, heavy saucepan, heat about 2 inches of oil to 350F (180C) or until a 1-inch bread cube turns golden brown in about 65 seconds. Add seafood-topped bread, a few triangles at a time; cook until golden on all sides, turning occasionally. Drain on paper towels. Garnish with Italian parsley if desired. Makes 24.

— ANCHOVY BEIGNETS —

¼ cup butter, cut in pieces
½ cup water
½ cup all-purpose flour
4 canned flat anchovy fillets, drained, mashed
2 eggs
2 tablespoons slivered almonds
Vegetable oil for deep-frying

In a medium saucepan, heat water and butter until melted, stirring; bring to a fast boil.

Add flour all at once. Stir over a low heat for about 1 minute or until mixture leaves sides and forms a ball; remove from heat and cool slightly. Beat in anchovy fillets, then beat in eggs, 1 at a time, beating until smooth after each addition. Stir in slivered almonds.

In a deep, heavy saucepan, heat about 2 inches of oil to 375F (190C) or until a 1-inch bread cube turns golden brown in about 50 seconds. Add a few teaspoons of the anchovy mixture at a time, and cook until golden on all sides. Drain on paper towels. Serve warm. Provide small napkins. Makes 12 to 15.

- ARTICHOKES WITH CAVIAR -

**1 (14 oz.) can artichoke bottoms packed in
    water**
3 to 6 slices firm-textured bread
2 tablespoons vegetable oil
2 tablespoons dairy sour cream
**1 tablespoon Aioli, page 93, or mayonnaise,
    preferably homemade**
Lemon juice to taste
1 tablespoon chopped chives
2 tablespoons black or red caviar
Dill sprigs if desired

Drain artichoke bottoms in a sieve;
pat dry with paper towels. Cut bread
slices into 2½-inch rounds; you will
need 6 bread rounds. Reserve bread
trimmings for bread crumbs or other
uses, if desired.

Heat oil in a skillet, add bread rounds
and cook, turning as needed, until
golden on both sides. Drain on paper
towels. If prepared ahead, cool; then
store in an airtight container up to 24
hours.

In a bowl, stir together sour cream,
Aioli or mayonnaise, lemon juice and
chives. Cover and refrigerate until
ready to serve. To assemble, arrange 1
artichoke bottom on each toasted
bread round. Top each with a spoonful
of the sour-cream mixture and 1 teaspoon caviar. If desired, garnish with
dill sprigs. Makes 6.

CAVIAR MOLDS

½ lb. black caviar, drained, rinsed
2 teaspoons unflavored gelatin
½ cup cold water
1¼ cups dairy sour cream
3 green onions, finely chopped
Quail eggs or hard-cooked hen eggs, if desired
Fresh fennel sprigs and Italian parsley

Place caviar in a bowl. In a small saucepan, soften gelatin in cold water; then place over low heat and stir until gelatin is dissolved. Stir dissolved gelatin into caviar.

Divide mixture evenly among 4 individual ½-cup molds or pour into a 2-cup mold. Refrigerate until set or up to 24 hours (this dish is best made no earlier than 1 day before serving). Meanwhile, in a small bowl, stir together sour cream and green onions; cover and refrigerate. If using quail eggs for garnish, boil 5 minutes, then cool and remove shells.

To serve, dip each mold up to rim in hot water; invert onto a platter. Lift off molds. If desired, garnish with lemon wedges and quail eggs or hard-cooked hen eggs. If using hen eggs, cut decorative shapes from the whites; press yolks through a sieve. Arrange egg-white shapes on molds; place the sieved yolks in the center. Serve with sour cream mixture. Makes four ½-cup molds or one 2-cup mold.

– HERB & GARLIC MUSSELS –

2 lbs. mussels in-the-shell
½ cup butter, room temperature
2 garlic cloves, crushed
2 tablespoons chopped parsley
1 tablespoon chopped chives
1 tablespoon chopped fresh dill

Scrub mussels well with a stiff brush. Pull out and discard beards. Then soak mussels several hours in cold water to cover; discard any mussels with broken shells. Drain well.

In a large saucepan, bring 2 cups water to a boil. Add as many mussels as will fit in a single layer; boil until shells open, then remove from pan. Repeat with remaining mussels, adding uncooked mussels as cooked ones are removed. Lift off and discard top shell of each mussel. Discard any mussels that do not open.

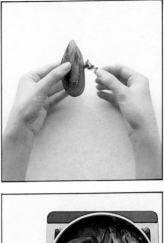

In a bowl, beat butter, garlic, parsley, chives and dill until well blended. Spread mixture evenly over mussels. Cover and refrigerate until ready to cook. To cook, preheat broiler. Arrange mussels in a broiler pan; broil until tops are lightly browned. Serve hot. Makes about 30, depending on size of mussels.

CUCUMBER WITH MUSSELS

1 (about 3½-oz.) can smoked mussels or oysters
1 teaspoon lemon juice
Few drops of hot-pepper sauce
4 oz. cream cheese, cut in chunks
3 tablespoons finely chopped celery
1 English cucumber
Red Salmon caviar and small dill sprigs, if
   desired

Drain mussels or oysters. Place drained mussels or oysters in a food processor fitted with a metal blade. Add lemon juice, hot-pepper sauce and cream cheese. Process until well blended. Turn mixture into a bowl; stir in celery. Cover and refrigerate until ready to serve.

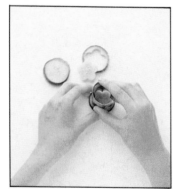

To serve, cut cucumber crosswise in ½-inch-thick slices. Then cut out each slice with a fluted cookie or hors d' oeuvres cutter; scoop a little flesh from center of each cutout.

Spoon mussel or oyster mixture evenly onto cucumber cutouts; top with caviar and dill sprigs, if desired. Serve immediately. Makes about 30.

— OYSTERS WITH CAVIAR —

36 oysters on-the-half-shell
2 tablespoons mayonnaise or dairy sour cream
1 teaspoon tomato paste
Salt, pepper and lemon juice to taste
2 to 3 teaspoons prepared horseradish
3 to 4 tablespoons black caviar
Small dill sprigs

Arrange oysters on rimmed serving plates or a platter (if desired, nest oysters in a bed of ice). Set aside.

In a small bowl, stir together mayonnaise or sour cream and tomato paste. Season with salt, pepper and lemon juice. Stir in enough horseradish to give a definite horseradish flavor.

Spoon a little horseradish sauce atop each oyster, then top each oyster with 1/3 to 1/2 teaspoon caviar and a dill sprig. Or, if desired, serve sauce and caviar in separate bowls for spooning over oysters. Provide small forks and napkins. Makes 36.

— OYSTERS ROCKEFELLER —

36 oysters on-the-half-shell
1 (10-oz.) pkg. frozen chopped spinach, thawed
1¼ cups dairy sour cream
2 garlic cloves, crushed
Salt and freshly ground pepper to taste
3 tablespoons finely shredded Cheddar cheese
½ cup soft bread crumbs
Italian parsley

Remove oysters from their shells; set oysters and shells aside. Drain spinach well, then place in a sieve and press out as much water as possible.

Place spinach in a bowl; stir in sour cream and garlic. Season with salt and pepper. Place about 1 teaspoon spinach mixture in each shell.

Return oysters to shells. Spoon remaining spinach mixture over oysters. Preheat broiler. Arrange oysters in a broiler pan; mix cheese and bread crumbs and sprinkle evenly over oysters. Broil until cheese is melted and crumbs are golden. Garnish with Italian parsley. Serve hot; provide small forks and napkins. Makes 36.

— ANGELS ON HORSEBACK —

24 shucked fresh oysters or 2 (8- or 10-oz.) jars
  oysters, drained
Juice of ½ lemon
1 tablespoon Worcestershire sauce
Freshly ground pepper to taste
3 or 4 thin bacon slices

Place oysters in a large bowl. Squeeze in the lemon juice, add Worcestershire sauce and pepper. Cover and refrigerate at least 1 hour.

Cut bacon slices lengthwise in ½-inch-wide strips; then cut strips crosswise in pieces long enough to wrap around an oyster. (Reserve any bacon trimmings for other uses, if desired.)

Secure bacon around oysters with wooden picks. Refrigerate until ready to serve. To serve, preheat broiler. Arrange bacon-wrapped oysters in a broiling pan and broil until bacon is crisp. Or preheat oven to 400F (200C); bake oysters 10 minutes or until bacon is crisp. Cool slightly before serving; be sure to provide napkins. Makes 24.

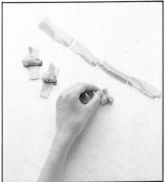

SPANISH SHRIMP

1 lb. uncooked jumbo shrimp
6 tablespoons olive oil; or 3 tablespoons olive
 oil and 3 tablespoons vegetable oil
1 or 2 small, fresh hot chilies, seeded, cut in
 slivers
3 garlic cloves, crushed

Remove shells from shrimp; remove
heads, but leave on tails. Cut each
shrimp down center of back, cutting
about halfway through so shrimp
curls; rinse out and vein. Set aside.

Pour oil into a large skillet; stir in
chilies. Place over a medium-high
heat. When oil is very hot, add shrimp
and garlic. Cook, stirring, until
shrimp turn pink. Serve immediately,
with crusty bread, lemon wedges and
Tartar Sauce. Makes 4 servings.

TARTAR SAUCE:

6 tablespoons mayonnaise, preferably
 homemade
3 green onions, chopped
1 tablespoon drained capers
1 tablespoon chopped sweet pickle
1 tablespoon chopped parsley

In a bowl, stir together mayonnaise,
green onions, capers, pickle and parsley. Cover and refrigerate until ready
to serve.

GRILLED SHRIMP

8 uncooked large or jumbo shrimps
1 teaspoon vegetable oil
2 tablespoons soy sauce
2 tablespoons dry sherry
½ teaspoon shredded fresh gingerroot
Squeeze of lemon juice
Lemon slices and fresh fennel sprigs

Remove heads from shrimp, but leave on tails. Then cut each shrimp through shell down center of back; be careful not to cut shrimp all the way through. Rinse out sand vein.

Gently spread each shrimp out flat; then thread each one on a metal or bamboo skewer, keeping shrimp lying flat. Set shrimp aside. In a small bowl, stir together oil, soy sauce, sherry, gingerroot and lemon juice.

Arrange skewered shrimp in a large skillet over medium heat. Cook, brushing frequently with soy-sauce mixture and turning several times, until shrimp are pink and well glazed. (Or broil shrimp until done, basting frequently.) Serve whole or cut in pieces; accompany with lemon slices and fresh fennel. Makes 8.

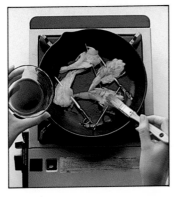

— SUSHI WITH SHRIMP —

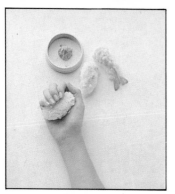

1 lb. short-grain rice
2 tablespoons mirin (sweet sake)
¼ cup rice vinegar
2 tablespoons sugar
2 teaspoons salt
24 cooked large shrimp
2 teaspoons wasabi powder
Nori (dried laver seaweed), if desired

Wash the rice several times in cold water and allow to drain well for 30 minutes. Put into a saucepan with the cold water. Bring to the boil, cover and steam over very low heat for 15 minutes. Heat mirin, vinegar, sugar and salt until boiling. Cool.

Remove rice from the heat and leave for 10 minutes. Turn rice into a large shallow dish and pour the vinegar dressing over. Mix gently but thoroughly until the rice reaches room temperature.

Shape the sushi into neat ovals and place on a serving platter. Peel the prawns, removing heads and leaving on the tails. Split down the underside – not all the way through – and flatten out. Wasabi is a very hot horseradish powder available from Asian food stores. Mix the powder with a few drops of water. Dab a little on the rice ovals and top each with a prawn. Wrap a strip of seaweed around each sushi if desired. *Makes 24.*

— CELERY WITH SHRIMP —

1¼ cups dairy sour cream
1 tablespoon drained capers, chopped
1 tablespoon chopped chives
2 tablespoons Dijon-style mustard
1 lb. cooked medium shrimp, shelled, deveined
3 or 4 celery stalks (be sure to use crisp,
  well-chilled celery)

Drain any liquid from the sour cream, and if the cream is thin, whip it until it thickens. Stir in the capers, chives and mustard. Cover and refrigerate until ready to serve.

Cut larger shrimp in halves or thirds; leave smaller ones whole.

Trim leafy tops and bases from celery stalks; remove any tough stems Cut each stalk crosswise in 2-inch lengths. Trim base of each length of celery so it will sit flat. Spoon sour-cream mixture evenly into celery; top with shrimp. Serve immediately. Makes about 18.

— SHRIMP VOL-AU-VENTS —

2 tablespoons butter
2 tablespoons all-purpose flour
1¼ cups milk
½ cup chopped cooked, shelled, deveined
   shrimps
Squeeze of lemon juice
Pinch of red (cayenne) pepper
1 teaspoon paprika
2 teaspoons chopped chives
Salt to taste
36 oyster cases (miniature puff-pastry shells)
Dill sprigs

Melt butter in a saucepan over low heat. Stir in flour; cook, stirring constantly, 2 minutes. Remove from heat, add milk all at once, stirring constantly.

Return to the heat and continue to cook, stirring, until sauce boils and thickens. Remove from heat. Stir in shrimps, lemon juice, red pepper, paprika and chives. Season with salt. Cool slightly. Preheat oven to 400F (200C).

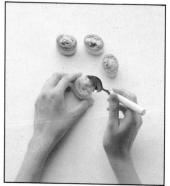

Fill oyster cases evenly with shrimp mixture. Arrange on baking sheets and bake 10 minutes. If vol-au-vents are extremely hot, cool slightly before serving. Garnish with dill sprigs. Provide small napkins. Makes 36.

CAVIAR CROUTONS

10 slices firm-textured white bread
2 tablespoons butter
2 tablespoons vegetable oil
1 to 2 teaspoons prepared horseradish,
**   or to taste**
½ cup dairy sour cream
3 tablespoons red salmon caviar
Small parsley sprigs, if desired

To make croutons, cut 2 shapes from each bread slice. Cut hearts with cookie or hors d'oeuvres cutters; cut diamonds with a knife. Reserve bread trimmings for breadcrumbs or other uses.

Melt butter in oil in a medium skillet. When fat is hot, add bread shapes. Cook, turning as needed, until golden on both sides. Drain on paper towels. If prepared ahead, cool; then store in an airtight container up to 24 hours. In a small bowl, stir together horse-radish and sour cream.

Just before serving, spoon sour-cream mixture onto croutons and top with caviar. If desired, garnish each canapé with a parsley sprig. Makes 20.

TARAMASALATA

2 thick slices crusty bread (about 6 oz. total)
1 (4-oz.) jar tarama
1 garlic clove, crushed
1 tablespoon grated onion
1 egg yolk
2 to 3 tablespoons lemon juice
½ cup olive oil
1 ripe olive
Fresh chives
Crusty bread

Trim crusts from 2 thick bread slices. Then place bread in a bowl, pour in enough cold water to cover and let soak for 10 minutes. Squeeze out excess water.

Place soaked, squeezed bread in a food processor fitted with a metal blade. Process to crumb bread evenly. Remove crumbs from work bowl; add tarama, garlic and onion. Process until thoroughly mixed. With motor running, gradually add bread crumbs, processing until mixture is smooth. Add egg yolk and 1 tablespoon lemon juice; process until blended.

With motor running, gradually pour in oil, processing until mixture is very creamy. Season with 1 to 2 tablespoons lemon juice, according to taste. Cover and refrigerate until serving time. To serve, pour in a serving bowl and garnish with olive; accompany with crusty bread for dipping. Makes 8 to 10 servings.

SALMON MOUSSE

1 tender cucumber without too many seeds
1 (15½-oz.) can red salmon
1 tablespoon unflavored gelatin
½ cup cold water
½ teaspoon dry mustard
2 tablespoons distilled white vinegar
1 teaspoon paprika
½ pint whipping cream (1 cup)
Melba toast or rye wafers

Trim the cucumber ends. Thinly slice lengthwise. Line a long, narrow 2-cup loaf pan with cucumber slices.

Drain salmon. Discard skin and bones, then place salmon in a food processor fitted with a metal blade. Process until smooth. In a small saucepan, soften gelatin in cold water; then place over low heat and stir until gelatin is dissolved. Pour gelatin over puréed salmon; add mustard, vinegar and paprika. Process until smoothly blended. With motor running, pour in cream, processing only until well mixed.

Pour into cucumber-lined pan, cover and refrigerate until set. To serve, dip pan in hot water up to rim for a couple of seconds. Invert onto a platter and lift off pan. Cut in slices; accompany with melba toast or rye wafers. Place atop melba toast to serve. Makes 4 to 6 servings.

SALMON & AVOCADO MOUSSE

1 recipe Salmon Mousse, page 27, made without cucumber
1 recipe Avocado Mousse, page 115,

Prepare Salmon Mousse as directed on page 27, but omit cucumber and line a 3-cup loaf pan with plastic wrap Pour mousse into lined pan; it should come about halfway up sides of pan. Cover and refrigerate until beginning to set around edges.

Prepare Avocado Mousse and spoon into a large pastry bag fitted with a plain tip. Hold tip of bag at 1 end of loaf pan, below surface of Salmon Mousse; pipe in Avocado Mousse, gradually moving tip to other end of loaf pan as you pipe. Cover and refrigerate until set.

To serve, dip pan up to rim in hot water, then invert onto a platter. Lift off pan and wrap. Cut in slices and serve on small plates lined with lettuce leaves. Accompany with horseradish cream, if desired. Provide plates and small forks for eating. Makes 10 to 12 servings.

OPEN SALMON SANDWICHES

6 thin slices pumpernickel, light rye or dark rye bread
¼ cup butter, room temperature
Crisp chicory or lettuce leaves, torn in small pieces
½ lb. thinly sliced smoked salmon
Dill sprigs and lemon twists

Using a cookie cutter, cut each bread slice into a round. Spread rounds liberally with butter.

Top each round with chicory or lettuce, then with a folded smoked-salmon slice. Garnish each sandwich with a dill sprig and a lemon twist. Serve immediately; or cover and refrigerate until ready to serve (up to 1 hour). Makes 6.

VARIATION:
If desired, top each sandwich with a dab of dairy sour cream flavored with chopped fresh dill and chopped capers.

- SMOKED-SALMON QUICHES -

½ (17¼-oz.) pkg. frozen puff pastry, thawed
6 eggs
1½ cups whipping cream
½ teaspoon salt
Pinch of ground nutmeg
¼ lb. smoked salmon, chopped
Black caviar, smoked salmon and dill sprigs, if
  desired

Preheat oven to 400F (200C). Grease twenty-four 2-inch tart pans. Unfold pastry sheets; place one on a lightly floured board, roll out slightly and cut into 24 rounds. Fit pastry rounds into greased tart pans.

In a bowl, beat eggs, cream, salt and nutmeg until blended. Stir in ¼ pound chopped salmon. Spoon mixture into the pastry-lined pans, making sure salmon is evenly distributed.

Bake 10 to 15 minutes or until filling is puffed and golden. Carefully remove from pans; if desired, garnish with caviar, titbits of salmon and dill sprigs. Serve warm. If prepared ahead, remove quiches from pans, cool completely on racks, cover and refrigerate. To reheat, arrange on baking sheets; bake in a 400F (200C) oven about 5 minutes or until heated through. Garnish. Makes 24.

SALMON CANAPÉS

1 (7½-oz.) can red salmon
½ teaspoon paprika
1 tablespoon half and half
Freshly ground pepper to taste
2 slices pumpernickel bread
2 tablespoons butter, room temperature
1 avocado
Lemon juice

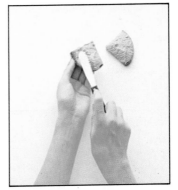

Drain salmon. Discard skin and bones. Place salmon in a bowl, add paprika and mix well, mashing salmon thoroughly. Gradually beat in half and half. Season with pepper. Cut the bread diagonally in quarters.

Spread 1 side of each triangle with butter. Pile salmon mixture evenly atop bread triangles, smoothing edges with a spatula.

Halve, pit and peel avocado. Slice each half lengthwise; cut each slice crosswise in small pieces. Arrange avocado evenly over salmon; sprinkle with lemon juice. Makes 8.

SALMON PUFFS

½ cup water
½ teaspoon salt
¼ cup butter, cut in pieces
½ cup all-purpose flour
¼ cup shredded Cheddar cheese (1 oz.)
2 eggs
1 (7½-oz.) can red salmon
2 tablespoons mayonnaise
1 tablespoon sliced pimento-stuffed green olives
Red and black caviar, if desired

Preheat oven to 400F (200C). Grease 2 baking sheets. Sift flour. In a saucepan, heat water, salt and butter until butter is melted stirring constantly. Bring mixture to a full boil.

Add flour all at once. Stir over low heat about 1 minute or until mixture leaves sides of pan and forms a ball. Remove from heat, stir in cheese and cool slightly. Beat in eggs, 1 at a time, beating until smooth after each addition.

Drop batter by teaspoonfuls onto greased baking sheets. Bake about 20 minutes or until puffy and golden. Remove from baking sheets; cool on racks. Cut each puff in half; scoop out any soft centers. Drain salmon. Discard skin and bones. Place salmon in a bowl; flake with a fork and mix in mayonnaise and olives. Fill puffs with salmon mixture; if desired, dip in caviar. Serve immediately. Makes about 25.

SQUID RINGS

1 lb. tender squid
2 or 3 large lettuce leaves
2 sheets nori (dried laver seaweed), if desired
½ cup soy sauce
2 tablespoons water
2 tablespoons sugar

To clean squid, hold body in 1 hand and base of tentacles just above eyes in other hand. Pull gently to separate body and tentacles. Pull transparent pen from body; pull out and discard viscera and ink sac. Rinse body cavity. Pull off and discard transparent, speckled membrane covering larger squid. Cut off tentacles just above eyes; discard eyes. Squeeze beak from base of tentacles; discard beak. Rinse tentacles well.

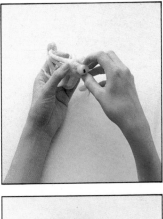

Place lettuce leaves in a bowl and pour in enough boiling water to cover. Drain well. Wrap tentacles tightly in lettuce leaves, then enclose in nori, if desired. If using nori, seal by wetting edges and pressing together.

Stuff tentacle bundle into squid body and fasten body closed with a skewer. In a large saucepan, mix soy sauce, water and sugar. Heat, stirring, until sugar is dissolved; add squid. Reduce heat, cover and simmer, turning occasionally, 20 to 30 minutes or until squid is tender when pierced with a skewer. Remove from heat. Cool, then refrigerate until cold. To serve, cut in slices. Makes about 20 slices.

PICKLED SQUID

1 lb. squid
6 tablespoons olive oil
3 tablespoons dry white wine
3 tablespoons white-wine vinegar
2 garlic cloves
Whole, red hot chilies
Salt and pepper to taste

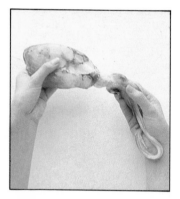

To clean squid, hold body in 1 hand and base of tentacles just above eyes in other hand. Pull gently to separate body and tentacles. Pull out transparent pen from body; pull out and discard viscera and ink sac. Rinse body cavity. Pull off speckled membrane covering larger squid.

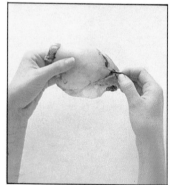

Cut off tentacles just above eyes; discard eyes. Squeeze beak from base of tentacles. Discard beak. Rinse tentacles well.

Drop squid tentacles and bodies into a saucepan full of boiling water. Return to a full boil; then drain squid, rinse under cold running water and drain again. Pat dry. Cut squid bodies crosswise in about ¾-inch-thick slices. Place slices in a large bowl; add oil, wine, vinegar, garlic, chilies, salt and pepper. Stir well. Cover and refrigerate at least 8 hours, stirring occasionally so flavors mingle. Lift squid from marinade and serve. Makes about 7 to 8 servings.

— CRISPY ALMOND SQUID —

1 lb. cleaned squid bodies (mantles)
½ cup all-purpose flour
Salt and pepper to taste
2 eggs
1 cup fine dry bread crumbs
½ cup finely chopped unblanched almonds
Vegetable oil for deep-frying

Slice squid bodies crosswise into rings. (If bodies alone are not available, buy 1 whole squid and clean as directed for Pickled Squid, page 34. Use bodies in this recipe; reserve tentacles for other uses.)

Combine flour, salt and pepper in a shallow dish. In another shallow dish, beat eggs to blend well. On a sheet of wax paper, mix bread crumbs and almonds. Roll squid in flour mixture, a few pieces at a time; dip in beaten eggs, then roll in crumb mixture to coat well. Arrange crumb-coated squid in a single layer on a baking sheet or flat platter. Cover and refrigerate until ready to cook.

To cook, in a deep, heavy saucepan, heat about 2 inches of oil to 375F (190C) or until a 1-inch bread cube turns golden brown in about 50 seconds. Add squid, a few pieces at a time, and cook just until golden on all sides; do not overcook or squid will toughen. Remove from oil with a slotted spoon and drain well on paper towels. Makes 4 to 8 servings.

— DEVILS ON HORSEBACK —

½ lb. prunes
About ¾ cup whole unblanched almonds
About 10 bacon slices
Hot mango chutney

Remove pits from prunes, then stuff each prune with an almond.

Cut each bacon slice in pieces, just long enough to wrap around stuffed prunes and overlap slightly; secure bacon around prunes with wooden picks.

To serve, preheat broiler. Arrange bacon-wrapped prunes in a broiler pan and broil until the bacon is crisp. Or preheat oven to 400F (200C) and bake 10 to 15 minutes until crisp. Serve with chutney. Makes 20 to 25.

—————————— TIP ——————————

Originally, "devils on horseback" meant prunes stuffed with hot chutney – hence the name "devil". For ease of preparation, though, we suggest stuffing the prunes with almonds and serving hot chutney alongside for dipping.

— BACON SANDWICHES —

½ lb. bacon slices
1 bunch watercress
24 slices firm-textured white or whole-wheat
**   bread (or use some white bread, some**
**   whole-wheat bread)**
6 tablespoons butter, room temperature
1 teaspoon Dijon-style mustard
Freshly ground pepper to taste

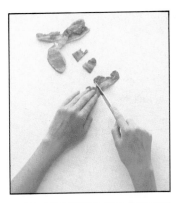

Broil bacon (or cook in a skillet) until crisp. Drain, cool and cut or break in small pieces. Set aside. Wash watercress in cold water; remove and discard tough stems. Shake watercress dry and separate into sprigs. Cover and refrigerate until ready to use.

Cut out each slice of bread with a round cookie cutter. Reserve bread trimmings for bread crumbs or other uses, if desired. In a small bowl, beat together butter and mustard; spread over 1 side of each bread round.

Evenly top buttered side of 12 bread rounds with bacon. Sprinkle with pepper, then top with watercress; top with remaining 12 bread rounds, buttered-side down. If preparing ahead, cover with plastic wrap and refrigerate a few hours. Makes 12.

BACON ROLLS

1 (8-oz.) can whole water chestnuts, drained
1 tablespoon soy sauce
1 teaspoon sugar
1 tablespoon dry white wine
1 (14-oz.) can artichoke hearts packed in water,
  drained
1 recipe Marinated Mushrooms (page 113)
18 to 21 bacon slices
Fresh chives, if desired

Place water chestnuts in a bowl with soy sauce, sugar and wine; stir well. Cover and let stand 30 minutes.

Rinse artichoke hearts well in cold water. Drain; pat dry. Cut any large artichoke hearts in halves or quarters. Drain mushrooms.

Preheat broiler. Cut bacon slices in pieces long enough to wrap around water chestnuts, artichokes and mushrooms. (You'll need 4 or 5 slices for water chestnuts, about 4 slices for artichokes and 10 to 12 slices for mushrooms.) Secure bacon around each water chestnut, artichoke and mushroom with wooden picks. Arrange bacon-wrapped food in a broiler pan; broil until bacon is crisp. Serve arranged on fresh chives, if desired. Makes about 50 (12 to 15 *each* water chestnuts and artichokes, about 24 mushrooms).

HAM CRESCENTS

4 oz. cream cheese, room temperature
½ cup butter, room temperature
1 cup all-purpose flour
½ lb. cooked ham, cut in chunks
1 teaspoon prepared hot mustard
2 tablespoons dairy sour cream
1 egg, beaten

In a bowl, beat cream cheese and butter until light and creamy. Blend in flour. Turn out dough onto a floured work surface; knead lightly. Wrap in plastic wrap and refrigerate until firm enough to handle. Meanwhile, place ham in a food processor fitted with a metal blade; process until finely minced. (Or mince ham with a knife.) Turn ham into a bowl and mix in mustard and sour cream. Cover and refrigerate until ready to use.

On a well-floured board, roll out pastry thinly. (Or dust 2 sheets of plastic wrap with flour; roll out pastry between floured sheets of plastic wrap.) Cut rolled-out dough into 3-inch rounds.

Preheat oven to 400F (200C). Place 1 heaping teaspoon of filling on each pastry round. Brush edges of each round with egg; fold pastry rounds in half over filling. Press edges with a fork to seal. Prick each pastry with tip of a sharp knife to allow steam to escape. Arrange pastries on baking sheets; bake 10 to 15 minutes or until golden. Serve hot. Makes 20 to 24.

— HAM & CHEESE CANAPÉS —

10 slices firm-textured white bread
¼ cup butter, room temperature
1 garlic clove, crushed
10 slices ham
10 slices Swiss or Gruyère cheese
Cherry tomatoes and basil sprigs

Toast bread until golden on both sides. While toast is still hot, cut each slice into a round using the rim of a glass.

In a small bowl, blend butter and garlic. Spread butter mixture on 1 side of each toast round. Cut ham and cheese slices to the same size as the toast rounds. Place 1 ham round, then 1 cheese round on each toast round. Reserve ham and cheese trimmings for use in pies, sandwich fillings or other dishes.

Preheat oven to 350F (180C). Arrange canapés on a baking sheet; bake 10 to 15 minutes or until cheese is melted. Top each canapé with a cherry tomato and basil. Serve hot. Makes 10.

— RIBBON SANDWICHES —

1 loaf firm-textured white bread (or use some
   white bread, some whole-wheat bread)
½ lb. cooked ham, cut in chunks
3 tablespoons dairy sour cream
2 to 3 teaspoons prepared mustard
2 teaspoons tomato paste
½ lb. skinned, boned, cooked chicken, cut in
   chunks
2 tablespoons mayonnaise
2 tablespoons chopped chives
1 teaspoon dried leaf tarragon
Salt and pepper to taste
½ cup butter, room temperature
Italian parsley, if desired

Cut the bread into 30 thin slices, then trim the crusts.

Place ham in a food processor fitted with a metal blade and process until minced. Turn into a bowl; stir in sour cream, mustard and tomato paste. Set aside. Process chicken in food processor until minced. Stir in mayonnaise, chives and tarragon; season with salt and pepper.

Spread 1 side of each slice with butter. Spread buttered side of 10 slices with ham mixture. Top with 10 more bread slices, buttered-side up; spread evenly with chicken mixture. Top with remaining 10 bread slices, buttered-side down. Wrap sandwiches in plastic wrap and refrigerate until ready to serve. To serve, cut each sandwich in 3 strips; arrange on a platter with Italian parsley, if desired. Makes 30.

- HOT CHEESE & HAM PUFFS -

½ cup plus 1 tablespoon all-purpose flour
½ cup water
½ teaspoon salt
¼ cup butter, cut in pieces
2 eggs
2 tablespoons butter
½ cup milk
3 tablespoons shredded Cheddar cheese
About ½ cup chopped cooked ham
3 tablespoons freshly grated Parmesan cheese

Preheat oven to 400F (200C). Grease 2 baking sheets. Sift ½ cup flour onto a sheet of waxed paper. Heat water, the salt and ¼ cup butter until butter melts.

Bring to a full boil; add sifted flour all at once. Stir over low heat about 1 minute or until mixture leaves sides of pan and forms a ball. Remove from heat; cool slightly. Beat in eggs, 1 at a time, beating until smooth after each addition. Drop batter by heaping tea-spoonfuls onto baking sheets. Bake 25 to 30 minutes or until puffy. Cool on racks. Cut each puff in half; scoop out soft centers. Melt 2 tablespoons butter over low heat. Stir in 1 tablespoon flour and milk. Continue to cook, stirring, until sauce thickens. Add Cheddar cheese and stir until melted, then stir in ham. Remove from heat; season.

Spoon into bottom halves of puffs, then replace tops. Arrange on baking sheets. Sprinkle with Parmesan cheese. Bake 5 minutes. Makes 20.

SPRING ROLLS

½ lb. lean boneless pork
2 tablespoons vegetable oil
1 small red bell pepper, seeded, cut in thin slices
4 green onions, chopped
¼ lb. fresh beansprouts
6 lettuce leaves, shredded
2 teaspoons cornstarch mixed with 1
  tablespoon water
1 tablespoon soy sauce
½ teaspoon sugar
20 spring-roll wrappers, thawed if frozen
Vegetable oil for deep-frying

Thinly slice pork, then cut slices crosswise in narrow strips.

Heat 2 tablespoons oil in a large skillet. Add pork and cook until no longer pink, stirring. Push to 1 side of pan; add pepper and onions. Cook, stirring, 3 minutes. Stir in beansprouts, lettuce and cornstarch and water mixture. Cook, stirring, until thick. Stir in soy sauce and sugar. Cool.

Fill spring-roll wrappers 1 at a time, keeping remaining wrappers covered with damp paper towels or plastic wrap to prevent drying. To fill each wrapper, place 2 tablespoons cooled filling in center. Fold 1 end over filling; then tuck in sides and roll up. Brush seams with water; press to seal. In a deep, heavy saucepan, heat about 2 inches of oil to 350F (180C) or until a 1-inch bread cube turns golden brown in about 65 seconds. Add spring rolls, a few at a time, and cook until golden. Drain. Makes 20.

— CHINESE DUMPLINGS —

1 (8-oz.) can bamboo shoots, drained
4 green onions
½ lb. lean ground pork
½ teaspoon grated fresh gingerroot
1 teaspoon salt
1 egg white
2 teaspoons soy sauce
About 20 won-ton skins
Tomato roses and Italian parsley, if desired
Plum sauce or chili sauce

Finely chop the drained bamboo shoots and the green onions. In a bowl, combine bamboo shoots, green onions, pork, ginger root, salt, egg white and soy sauce. Work with won-ton skins a few at a time, keeping remaining skins covered with damp paper towels or plastic wrap to prevent drying.

To shape each dumpling, place a heaping teaspoon of filling on 1 won-ton skin. Bring sides of skin up around filling; squeeze together so it looks like a money pouch.

To cook, arrange dumplings slightly apart in a bamboo steaming basket. Steam over boiling water 20 minutes. Arrange on a platter with tomato roses and Italian parsley, if desired. Serve with plum sauce or chili sauce for dipping. Makes about 20.

SPICY PORK ROLLS

½ lb. pork tenderloin
6 or 7 green onions
1 garlic clove, crushed
1 tablespoon dark soy sauce
1 tablespoon honey
1 tablespoon vegetable oil
1 tablespoon hoisin sauce
1 teaspoon grated fresh gingerroot

Trim any excess fat from pork, then cut crosswise in 20 slices.

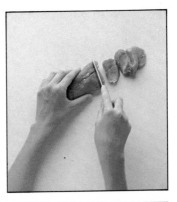

Flatten meat slices with a knife. Trim roots and any wilted leaves from green onions, then cut each onion in 3 or 4 pieces.

Roll each meat slice around 1 green-onion piece. (There's no need to fasten rolls closed – moisture in meat will keep them from coming open.) Preheat oven to 400F (200C). In a shallow baking dish, stir together garlic, soy sauce, honey, oil, hoisin sauce and gingerroot. Place pork rolls in soy mixture and turn to coat. If preparing ahead, cover and refrigerate. Bake, uncovered, 10 to 15 minutes or until meat is no longer pink in center; cut to test. During baking, baste rolls frequently with sauce. Serve hot or warm. Makes 20.

— SALAMI CRESCENTS —

1 (17¼-oz.) pkg. frozen puff pastry, thawed
2 tablespoons dairy sour cream
1 teaspoon prepared hot mustard
16 slices mettwurst salami
8 slices Swiss cheese, room temperature
1 egg, beaten

Unfold pastry sheets. On a lightly floured board, roll out each sheet of pastry to a 14-inch square. Cut each square in quarters, making a total of eight 7-inch squares.

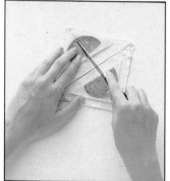

Preheat oven to 400F (200C). In a small bowl, mix sour cream and mustard. Spread evenly over pastry squares, spreading almost to edges of pastry. Cut each salami slice in half; cut each cheese slice diagonally in half. Arrange salami and cheese on pastry; cut each pastry square diagonally in half to make 2 triangles, then cut into quarters.

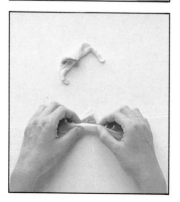

Starting from wide side, roll up each pastry triangle. Arrange on baking sheets, points underneath; bend pastries gently into crescent shapes. Brush with egg. Bake 10 to 15 minutes until golden. Makes 32.

— LIVERWURST CANAPÉS —

1 (about 12-inch-long) crusty baguette
3 tablespoons olive oil
2 tablespoons butter, melted
1 small garlic clove, crushed
6 thin slices Swiss cheese
½ lb. smoked liverwurst
Pickled sweet gherkins

Preheat oven to 400F (200C). Cut baguette in ½-inch-thick slices.

Stir together oil, melted butter and garlic; brush on both sides of bread slices. Arrange in a single layer in a baking dish. Bake 10 minutes or until bread is golden and crisp around edges. Meanwhile, cut each cheese slice in quarters; set aside. In a bowl, beat liverwurst until softened.

Spread liverwurst evenly on each slice of hot toast. Top each slice with 1 piece of cheese; return to oven and bake 5 to 10 minutes longer or until cheese is melted. Garnish each canapé with a pickled sweet gherkin and serve hot. Makes about 24.

— SATAY SAUSAGE ROLLS —

1 tablespoon vegetable oil
1 onion, finely chopped
1 tablespoon dark soy sauce
2 teaspoons lemon juice
2 garlic cloves, crushed
Hot sauce to taste
3 eggs
1½ lbs. pork sausagemeat
3 sheets frozen puff pastry (1½ x 17¼-oz. pkg.)
   thawed

Heat oil in a medium saucepan over a low heat. Add onion; cook until soft, stirring occasionally. Stir in soy sauce, lemon juice, garlic and sauce.

In a large bowl, thoroughly mix onion mixture, 2 eggs and sausage. Set aside. Preheat oven to 400F (200C). Unfold pastry sheets. Place on a lightly floured board and roll out slightly to make a 22″ x 10″ rectangle. Cut rectangle in two 11″ x 10″ strips; cut each strip in half lengthwise again to make four 5½″ x 10″ strips.

Spoon ¼ of sausage mixture down center of each pastry strip. Beat remaining egg; brush over edges of pastry strips. Fold pastry over filling; press to seal. Slash top of each pastry roll; cut each roll in 1- to 1½-inch lengths. Arrange on baking sheets; bake about 20 minutes or until golden. Serve hot with spicy sauce. Makes about 40.

LIVERWURST BALLS

2 bacon slices
1 small onion, finely chopped
½ lb. liverwurst
2 tablespoons brandy or orange-flavored
   liqueur
About 1 cup chopped parsley
Orange slices and orange peel strips, if desired

Cut the bacon slices in fine dice. In a skillet, cook bacon over low heat, stirring, until it begins to turn crisp. Remove bacon from pan. Add onion to dripping in pan; cook over low heat, stirring until soft.

In a large bowl, combine bacon, onion and liverwurst; mix well. Warm brandy or liqueur in a small saucepan. Carefully ignite; pour over liverwurst mixture and let flame die down. Mix well. Cover and refrigerate until firm.

Spread parsley on a sheet of waxed paper. Roll chilled liverwurst mixture into balls, a heaping teaspoonful at a time then roll in parsley to coat well. Arrange on a plate, cover and refrigerate until ready to serve. If desired, garnish with orange slices and orange peel strips. Makes 12 to 15.

BARBECUED CSABAI

**2 pairs hot or original (mild) csabai sausage
(*not* csabai salami, which is much harder)**

Cut csabai into about 3-inch lengths and peel off skin.

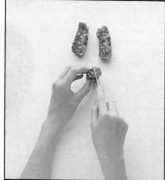

Then split each piece of csabai in half lengthwise. Cover and refrigerate until ready to cook.

To cook, arrange sausage pieces, cut sides down, on a lightly greased grill about 4 inches above a solid bed of glowing coals. (Or cook in a large skillet over medium heat.) Cook, turning as needed, until browned on all sides. Cut in chunks and serve hot. Makes 40-60 pieces.

————————— TIP —————————

This appetizer is an ideal beginning for a barbecue meal – not only do the sausages taste delicious, but their flavor penetrates the meats cooked for the main course. If you don't want to barbecue the sausage, you may broil or pan-fry it.

— PIROSHKI WITH THYME —

2 oz. fresh yeast
2 tablespoons sugar
¾ cup warm milk (110F, 45C)
3 cups all-purpose flour
2 teaspoooons salt
¾ cup butter
3 large onions, chopped
½ lb. bacon slices, finely chopped
1 teaspoon pepper
2 tablespoons fresh thyme leaves
1 egg, beaten

Cream yeast with sugar. Stir in milk.

In a bowl, stir together flour and salt. Stir in yeast mixture and ½ cup melted butter. Beat to mix well; then beat vigorously about 3 minutes to make a smooth batter. Cover with plastic wrap and let rise in a warm place about 1 hour or until doubled. Melt remaining ¼ cup butter in a large skillet. Add onions and cook until soft and golden, stirring frequently; cool. Stir in bacon, pepper and thyme.

Punch down dough. Turn out onto a lightly floured board and knead briefly, then divide into 35 to 40 equal portions. Wrap a spoonful of filling in each portion of dough. Grease 2 or 3 baking sheets; arrange piroshki on baking sheets and let rise in a warm place 15 minutes. Brush piroshki with egg. Preheat oven to 450F (230C). Bake 10 to 15 minutes or until golden. Makes 35 to 40.

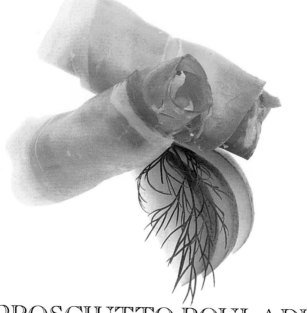

— PROSCIUTTO ROULADES —

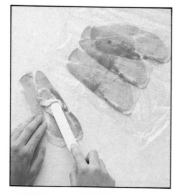

2 oz. ricotta cheese (¼ cup)
2 oz. Stilton cheese, crumbled
1 tablespoon dairy sour cream
12 very thin slices prosciutto, coppa salami or
lean cooked ham
1 pear
Lemon juice
Lime slices and dill sprigs, if desired

In a small bowl, thoroughly blend ricotta cheese, Stilton cheese and sour cream. Spread evenly on prosciutto, salami or ham slices, spreading mixture almost to edges.

Peel, quarter and core pear, then cut each quarter lengthwise in 3 thin slices. Brush slices lightly with lemon juice to prevent darkening. Place a pear slice on each cheese-topped prosciutto slice.

Roll up prosciutto slices, cover and refrigerate until ready to serve. Garnish with lime slice and dill sprig, if desired. Makes 12.

VARIATION:
Substitute an apple or fresh figs for the pear. Peel and slice figs before using.

RUMAKI

1 lb. chicken livers
2 tablespoons vegetable oil
1 tablespoon soy sauce
1 tablespoon dry sherry
Squeeze of lemon juice
1 garlic clove, crushed
About 12 bacon slices
10 canned water chestnuts, drained, sliced

Rinse chicken livers, pat dry and cut each liver in half. Then cut out any dark spots, large veins and membranes. Heat oil in a large skillet over medium-low heat. Add livers, a portion at a time; cook, turning constantly, just until livers are no longer red on outside.

Remove skillet from heat. Return all livers to skillet, then mix in soy sauce, sherry, lemon juice and garlic. Cool completely. Cut each bacon slice in halves or thirds.

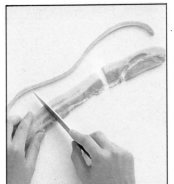

Place 1 piece of chicken liver on 1 bacon piece; top with a slice of water chestnut. Roll bacon around livers and water chestnuts; secure with a wooden pick. Repeat with remaining bacon, livers and water chestnuts. Cover and refrigerate until ready to cook. To cook, preheat broiler. Arrange rumaki in a broiler pan; broil until crisp. Serve hot. Makes about 28.

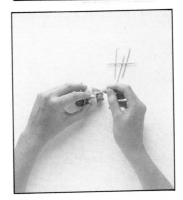

CHICKEN & SAUSAGE ROLLS

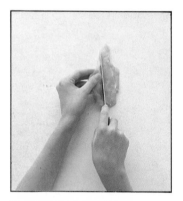

1 lb. skinned, boned chicken breasts
Salt and pepper to taste
2 or 3 pepperoni sausages
12 green beans, ends and strings removed
6 sheets filo pastry
½ cup butter, melted

Slice the chicken in half to make 2 thin breasts; place between sheets of plastic wrap and pound with a flat-surfaced mallet to make a thin, even layer. Sprinkle with salt and pepper. Divide pounded chicken into 6 portions.

Peel skin from pepperoni and cut in pieces about the same length as chicken portions (you'll need 6 pieces of pepperoni). Place 1 sausage piece in center of each chicken portion; place 2 green beans alongside each piece of pepperoni. Roll chicken around pepperoni and beans. Preheat oven to 400F (200C). Work with 1 sheet of pastry at a time, keeping remaining pastry covered with damp paper towels or plastic wrap to prevent drying. To shape each roll, brush 1 sheet of pastry with butter; fold in quarters.

Place 1 chicken roll in center of folded pastry sheet; tuck in sides and roll up. Place rolls in shallow-rimmed baking pan; brush with remaining melted butter. Bake 15 to 20 minutes or until golden and crisp. Cut each roll in about 5 chunks; serve hot. Makes 30.

CHICKEN SATAY

1 lb. skinned, boned chicken breasts
½ teaspoon sambal oelek (hot-pepper paste)
1 teaspoon grated fresh gingerroot
2 tablespoons lemon juice
3 tablespoons dark soy sauce
2 tablespoons honey
1 tablespoon peanut butter
½ cup water
Cherries and Italian parsley, if desired

Cut chicken in 1-inch chunks and thread chunks equally on 15 bamboo skewers. Set aside.

In a large saucepan or skillet combine sambal oelek, gingerroot, lemon juice, soy sauce, honey, peanut butter and water. Bring to a boil, stirring constantly, then reduce heat and add as many chicken skewers as will fit without crowding. Simmer 10 minutes, basting. Remove from pan and transfer to a rimmed platter. Repeat with remaining chicken skewers.

Simmer sauce remaining in pan until reduced to about ¾ cup. Pour over chicken. Cover and refrigerate until cold, then serve. If desired garnish with cherries and Italian parsley. Makes 15.

SESAME CHICKEN

1 lb. skinned, boned chicken breasts
1 teaspoon salt
2 tablespoons light soy sauce
2 tablespoons maple syrup
2 tablespoons dry sherry
½ teaspoon shredded fresh gingerroot
½ teaspoon Chinese five-spice
2 tablespoons vegetable oil
2 tablespoons sesame seeds
Italian parsley
Chutney or plum sauce, if desired

Cut each breast in half lengthwise.

In a shallow baking dish, stir together salt, soy sauce, maple syrup, sherry, gingerroot, five-spice and oil. Add chicken and turn to coat evenly. Cover and refrigerate at least 2 hours or up to 8 hours, turning occasionally.

Preheat oven to 400F (200C). Sprinkle chicken with sesame seeds. Bake, uncovered, about 15 minutes or until no longer pink in thickest part; cut to test. Brush occasionally with marinade during baking. Cut chicken in chunks and serve warm or cold, garnished with Italian parsley. If desired, accompany with chutney or plum sauce. Makes about 24 pieces.

YAKITORI

½ lb. skinned, boned chicken breast
6 green onions
2 tablespoons sake
2 tablespoons light soy sauce
½ teaspoon grated fresh gingerroot
2 teaspoons sugar

Cut chicken in small cubes. Trim roots and any wilted leaves from green onions, then cut each onion in 1½-inch lengths, using some tops.

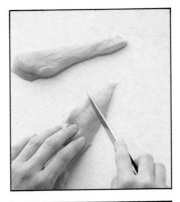

Thread chicken alternatively with green onions on 6 bamboo skewers.

Preheat broiler. In a small saucepan, heat sake; stir in soy sauce, gingerroot and sugar. Remove from heat. Place skewers in a broiler pan; cover any exposed bamboo at ends of skewers with foil. Brush sake mixture over skewers. Broil, brushing often with marinade and turning occasionally, about 6 minutes, or until chicken is no longer pink in center; cut to test. Serve hot. Makes 6.

— CHICKEN & LEEK ROLLS —

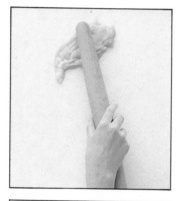

¾ lb. skinned, boned chicken breast
3 tablespoons dark soy sauce
1 tablespoon dry sherry
¼ tablespoon shredded fresh gingerroot
2 teaspoons sugar
2 leeks
2 tablespoons vegetable oil
½ cup water

Pound chicken with a rolling pin to make a thin, even layer. Divide chicken into 8 equal portions. In a shallow dish, stir together 2 tablespoons soy sauce, sherry, gingerroot and sugar. Set chicken and marinade aside.

Trim roots and tops of leeks, then cut leeks in quarters and wash thoroughly to remove sand. Arrange each leek quarter in center of 1 portion of chicken, wrap meat around leek. Secure with a skewer. Arrange chicken rolls in marinade, turn to coat, cover and refrigerate about 30 minutes.

Heat oil in a large skillet. Add chicken rolls and brown on all sides. Stir in remaining 1 tablespoon soy sauce and water. Cover and simmer 10 minutes or until chicken is tender. Lift from pan, remove skewers and cut each chicken roll in about 4 chunks. Serve hot or cold. Makes about 32.

– CHICKEN-PISTACHIO PÂTÉ –

½ lb. chicken livers
2 cups water
½ cup plus 2 tablespoons butter
1 small onion, chopped
1 garlic clove, chopped
2 tablespoons cognac
2 tablespoons whipping cream
½ cup plus 2 tablespoons pistachio nuts
Hot toast or crackers

Rinse livers and pat dry. Cut out any dark spots, large veins and membranes. Pour water into a saucepan and bring to a boil. Add livers, reduce heat, cover and simmer 5 minutes. Drain and set aside.

Melt ¼ cup butter in a skillet over medium-low heat. Add onion and garlic. Cook, stirring, until onion is soft but not browned. Add drained livers; cook, stirring, until livers are cooked through. Remove from heat and cool about 10 minutes. In a food processor fitted with a metal blade, process liver mixture until smooth. Melt ¼ cup butter; add to puréed liver mixture with cognac and cream. Process until blended. Stir in ½ cup pistachios.

Pour into 4 to 6 individual ramekins and refrigerate until cold. Melt remaining 2 tablespoons butter; pour evenly over pâté to make a thin layer. Sprinkle remaining 2 tablespoons pistachios over pâté. Refrigerate until ready to serve. Serve with toast or crackers. Makes 4 to 6 servings.

– GLAZED CHICKEN WINGS –

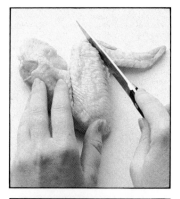

1½ lb. chicken wings
3 green onions, cut in 2-inch pieces
3 tablespoons dry sherry
¼ cup dark soy sauce
2 teaspoons sugar
Sesame seeds, if desired

With a sharp knife, remove the tips from the chicken wings. (These can be used for making stock, if desired.) The wings may be left whole or cut in two pieces at the joint.

Place the green onions in a large wok or pan over medium heat; stir in dry sherry and soy sauce; add sugar and bring to a full boil. Reduce heat and place chicken wings in soy sauce mixture.

Cover and simmer over a low heat for 20 minutes, turning occasionally, or until the chicken is no longer pink in the center; cut to test. If desired, sprinkle with sesame seeds. Serve warm or cold. Provide small napkins. Makes 8 to 10.

—— SMOKED-BEEF TARTS ——

1 cup all-purpose flour
Pinch of salt
1 tablespoon grated Parmesan cheese
¼ cup firm butter
1 egg, beaten
1 (14-oz.) can artichoke hearts, drained
¼ lb. thinly sliced smoked beef
2 tablespoons dairy sour cream
2 teaspoons chopped fresh dill
1 red pepper, cored, seeded, cut in thin strips

In a bowl, stir together flour, salt and cheese. Cut in butter until mixture resembles coarse crumbs. Add egg all at once; stir with a fork until dough holds together. Gather into a ball, wrap and refrigerate 30 minutes.

Lightly grease about 15 small tart pans. Dust 2 sheets of plastic wrap with flour. Roll out pastry thinly between sheets of floured plastic wrap. Peel off top sheet; cut pastry into about 15 rounds and fit into greased tart pans. Refrigerate 15 to 20 minutes. Preheat oven to 400F (200C). Prick pastry shells all over and bake 10 to 15 minutes, until golden. Cool on racks, then remove from pans.

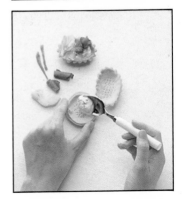

Rinse artichoke hearts well in cold water. Drain, pat dry. Cut in quarters. Cut beef slices in strips and roll each into a cylinder. Stir together sour cream and dill. To assemble, spoon a little of the mixture into each shell. Top with artichokes and beef. Cut each red pepper strip in half crosswise and add to the tarts. Makes about 15.

MINTED MEATBALLS

2 lbs. lean ground beef
3 eggs, beaten
2 onions, finely chopped
1½ cups soft bread crumbs
3 tablespoons lemon juice
2 tablespoons chopped fresh mint
2 garlic cloves, crushed
2 teaspoons salt
Vegetable oil for frying

Combine all the ingredients, except oil, and form into 40 balls with slightly wet hands.

Heat about ½ inch of oil in a large skillet. Add as many meatballs as will fit without crowding; cook, turning as needed, until well browned on all sides and cooked through. Remove from pan, drain on paper towels and keep hot. Repeat with remaining meatballs. Serve hot, with Minted Yogurt Sauce for dipping. The meatballs can be successfully cooked ahead and frozen. To reheat, arrange thawed meatballs on a baking sheet; bake in a 350F (180C) oven until heated through. Makes 40.

MINTED YOGURT SAUCE

6 green onions, finely chopped
8 oz. plain yogurt (1 cup)
3 tablespoons chopped fresh mint
2 teaspoons grated fresh gingerroot
1 garlic clove, crushed

In a bowl, stir together green onions and yogurt. Stir in chopped mint, gingerroot and garlic. Cover and refrigerate. Makes about 1 cup.

— OPEN BEEF SANDWICHES —

1 cup butter
2 teaspoons dried leaf tarragon
4 egg yolks
1 tablespoon distilled white vinegar
1 teaspoon green peppercorns
10 thick slices crusty French bread
About 1 lb. rare roast beef
Lettuce leaves, if desired

Melt butter with tarragon in a small saucepan; keep very hot. Process egg yolks in a food processor fitted with a metal blade until frothy. With motor running, pour in hot melted butter in a thin stream, process until mixed.

Add vinegar and process until combined. Stir in peppercorns by hand. Cover and refrigerate until cold or up to 1 week. (Unlike the traditional bèarnaise sauce, this sauce needs to be chilled before serving; the texture actually improves upon chilling.)

Cut the roast beef in 20 thin slices. Top each bread slice with lettuce leaves, if desired. Then arrange 2 small beef slices atop each bread slice. Spoon a little sauce atop each sandwich. Serve as soon as possible, accompanied with any remaining sauce. Makes 10.

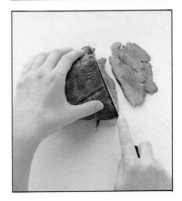

——————— TIP ———————

If preparing ahead, cover and refrigerate sauce; wrap bread slices and beef slices separately and refrigerate. Assemble sandwiches just before serving.

—CURRANT MEATBALLS—

1 cup soft white bread crumbs
½ cup half and half
1 lb. lean ground beef
1 small onion, finely chopped
½ teaspoon ground cinnamon
Pinch of ground cloves
1 egg, beaten
1 to 2 teaspoons salt
About ⅓ cup currants
About 6 tablespoons toasted pine nuts
About 2 tablespoons vegetable oil
Fresh mint sprigs

Soak bread crumbs in half and half about 5 minutes. In a bowl, thoroughly mix beef, onion, cinnamon, cloves, egg, salt, currants and toasted pine nuts. Then mix in soaked crumbs.

With wet hands, shape mixture into 20 equal balls.

Heat 2 tablespoons oil in a large skillet. Add as many meatballs as will fit without crowding. Cook, turning as needed, until well browned on all sides and cooked through. Remove from pan; keep hot. Repeat with remaining meatballs, adding more oil as needed. Serve hot. If prepared ahead, cover and refrigerate cooked meatballs. To reheat, arrange in a shallow baking dish; bake in 350F (180C) oven about 10 minutes or until heated through, garnish with mint sprigs and serve hot. Makes 20.

— SMOKED-BEEF CANAPÉS —

10 slices pumpernickel or dark rye bread
½ cup butter, room temperature
20 to 30 thin slices smoked beef
1 cup mayonnaise, preferably homemade
1 (3¼-oz.) can tuna, drained
Juice of ½ lemon
Drained capers
Thin white-onion slices, dill sprigs and lemon
twists

Cut each bread slice in half; spread 1 side of each piece with butter.

In a bowl, combine mayonnaise, drained tuna, lemon juice and 1 teaspoon capers; mix until thoroughly blended.

Arrange beef evenly atop buttered bread. Spoon sauce over beef. Garnish each canapé with a few capers, a few onion slices, a dill sprig and a lemon twist. If preparing ahead, cover and refrigerate buttered bread, beef and tuna sauce separately; assemble canapés just before serving. Makes 20.

CURRY PIES

1 tablespoon vegetable oil
1 onion, chopped
1 lb. lean ground beef
1 tablespoon curry powder
2 tablespoons distilled white vinegar
6 tablespoons water
1 teaspoon salt
2 tablespoons seedless golden raisins
2 teaspoons cornstarch
½ lb. short pastry
1 egg, beaten

Heat oil in large skillet. Add onion, then crumble in beef. Cook, stirring, 2 minutes. Add curry powder; cook, stirring, 1 more minute. Stir in vinegar, 4 tablespoons water, salt and raisins. Reduce heat, cover and simmer 10 minutes.

Stir together cornstarch and remaining 2 tablespoons water; stir into meat mixture. Cook, stirring, about 2 minutes. Remove from heat; cool, then refrigerate until cold.

Preheat oven to 400F (200C). Lightly grease 12 to 15 tart pans. On a lightly floured board, roll out ½ of pastry thinly. Cut into 12 to 15 rounds and fit into greased 2-inch tart pans. Spoon cold meat mixture into pastry shells. Roll out remaining pastry, cut into rounds and place on tarts; trim edges and press with a fork to seal. Brush tops of tarts with egg or water, then prick each several times. Bake about 15 minutes. Makes 12 to 15.

MUSHROOMS & BLUE CHEESE

12 to 14 small fresh mushrooms
4 oz. blue-veined cheese
4 oz. cream cheese, room temperature
1 tablespoon half and half
Pecan halves and parsley sprigs or basil leaves

Cut stems out of mushrooms, then wipe mushrooms with a cloth dipped in cold acidulated water (1½ teaspoons lemon juice or distilled white vinegar to 2 cups water). Reserve stems for other uses, if desired. Set mushrooms aside.

Crumble blue-veined cheese into a medium bowl. Add cream cheese; beat until mixture is smooth, then add half and half and beat until fluffy. Spoon into a pastry bag fitted with a star tip. If preparing ahead, refrigerate cheese mixture in pastry bag; also cover and refrigerate mushrooms.

To serve, arrange mushrooms, cap-side down, on a serving plate. Pipe cheese mixture into hollow of each mushroom; top each with a pecan half and a parsley sprig or a basil leaf. Makes 12 to 14.

CHEESE STRAWS

6 tablespoons butter, room temperature
¾ cup shredded Cheddar cheese (3 oz.)
1 cup all-purpose flour
1 teaspoon paprika
Red (cayenne) pepper to taste

In a medium bowl, cream butter until fluffy; beat in cheese. Blend in flour. Divide dough in thirds; wrap each portion in plastic wrap and refrigerate until firm enough to roll.

Preheat oven to 350F (180C). Roll out 1 portion of dough at a time, keeping remaining dough refrigerated. To roll out each portion of dough, dust 2 sheets of plastic wrap with flour; roll out dough between floured sheets of plastic wrap to about ⅛ inch thick. Peel off top sheet of plastic. Cut rolled-out dough in 4-inch long, ½-inch-wide strips. Hold each strip at both ends; twist in opposite directions so each strip has 2 twists. Arrange twists on ungreased baking trays.

Mix paprika and red pepper. Using a dry pastry brush, dab paprika mixture onto cheese straws. Bake 10 minutes or until golden brown around edges. Makes about 80.

--- TIP ---

Very short doughs like this one are much easier to roll out if you roll them between sheets of plastic wrap. (This is especially true in hot weather.)

CHEESE BITES

8 oz. Cheddar cheese
6 to 10 bacon slices
40 fresh sage or basil leaves

Cut cheese in 40 equal cubes. Cut bacon slices in pieces long enough to wrap around cheese cubes.

Wrap 1 sage or basil leaf around each cheese cube, then wrap in 1 piece of bacon. Secure with wooden picks. Lightly grease a large skillet; add as many bacon rolls as will fit without crowding. Cook over medium heat until bacon is crisp. Drain on paper towels. Repeat with remaining bacon rolls. Serve hot or warm; provide small napkins. Makes 40.

CHEESE AND PEPPERONI BITES
In place of sage or basil leaves, use small, thin pepperoni slices.

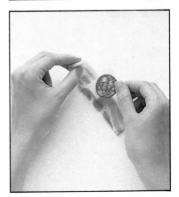

- CHEESE & ONION PASTRIES -

1½ cups (all-purpose) flour
½ teaspoon salt
½ cup cold water
2 tablespoons butter
1 cup chopped green onions including tops
About ⅛ teaspoon red (cayenne) pepper
4 oz. Gouda cheese
1 egg, beaten
Vegetable oil for deep-frying

In a bowl, stir together flour and salt. Then stir in cold water to make a firm dough. Turn out onto a lightly floured surface, knead until smooth. Wrap in plastic wrap; let rest 30 minutes.

Melt butter in a skillet; add green onions. Cook, stirring, until soft. Remove from heat and stir in red pepper. Set aside. Cut cheese in 24 equal cubes. Divide dough into 24 equal portions. On a lightly floured board, roll out each portion into a 4-inch round.

Spoon green-onion mixture evenly onto dough rounds, then top each round with a cheese cube. Brush edges of each round with egg; fold in half over filling and press edges with a fork to seal. In a deep, heavy saucepan, heat about 2 inches of oil to 350F (180C) or until a 1-inch bread cube turns golden brown in about 65 seconds. Add pastries, a few at a time, and cook until golden on all sides. Drain on paper towels and serve warm. Makes 24.

— SESAME CHEESE BALLS —

About ½ cup slivered almonds or pepitas
7 tablespoons sesame seeds
1 (8-oz.) pkg. cream cheese, room temperature
2 tablespoons grated Parmesan cheese
2 teaspoons instant minced onion
Salt and freshly ground pepper to taste
Tomato wedges and Italian parsley

Preheat oven to 350F (180C). Spread almonds on a baking sheet; bake about 10 minutes or until golden. Cool. Place sesame seeds in a dry skillet and stir over medium heat until golden. Remove from heat; cool.

In a bowl, beat together cream cheese, Parmesan cheese and onion. Season with salt and pepper. Cover with plastic wrap and refrigerate 20 minutes or until firm. Stir in cooled sesame seeds, then shape mixture into 25 equal balls.

Spread toasted almonds on a sheet of wax paper; roll cheese balls in nuts to coat. Arrange on a plate, cover and refrigerate (or keep in a cool place) until ready to serve. Garnish with tomato wedges and Italian parsley. Makes 25.

— ALMOND-CHEESE BALLS —

1 cup whole blanched almonds
2 cups finely shredded Cheddar cheese (8 oz.)
¼ cup all-purpose flour
2 egg whites
Vegetable oil for deep-frying

Coarsely chop almonds and spread on a piece of wax paper. In a bowl, lightly mix cheese and flour. In a large bowl, beat egg whites until stiff.

Sprinkle cheese-flour mixture over egg whites; gently fold together.

Form mixture into 16 to 18 equal balls. Roll cheese balls in almonds to coat; cover and refrigerate until ready to cook. To cook, in a deep, heavy saucepan, heat about 2 inches of oil to 350F (180C) or until a 1-inch bread cube turns golden brown in about 65 seconds. (Be sure oil is not too hot, or almonds will brown before centers of cheese balls are heated through.) Add cheese balls to hot oil, a few at a time, and cook until golden on all sides. Drain on paper towels and serve hot. Makes 16 to 18.

— PEPPER-CHEESE ROUNDS —

8 oz. Cheddar cheese
1 (8-oz.) pkg. cream cheese, room temperature
¼ cup dry sherry
6 tablespoons coarsely cracked pepper
Toast rounds and cooked, shelled, deveined
  shrimp
Tomato wedges

Finely shred Cheddar cheese into a large bowl; beat Cheddar cheese and cream cheese until smooth and well blended. Gradually beat in sherry. Cover and refrigerate until firm.

Divide chilled cheese mixture into 4 equal portions. Place each on a sheet of plastic wrap or wax paper and shape into a 2-inch log. (Or shape cheese into balls.)

Spread pepper on a sheet of plastic wrap or wax paper. Roll cheese logs in pepper to coat all sides, gently pressing pepper into cheese. Wrap individually and refrigerate until ready to serve. To serve, cut logs in about ⅜-inch-thick slices. Place each slice on a toast round and top with a shrimp. Or serve slices plain and garnish with tomato wedges. Makes about 20 slices.

— APRICOT-NUT CHEESE —

1 (8-oz.) pkg. cream cheese, room temperature
½ cup moist-pack dried apricots, cut in small
**   pieces**
6 tablespoons whole hazelnuts
¼ cup poppy seeds or toasted sesame seeds
Crackers or apple wedges, if desired
Italian parsley

In a bowl, beat cream cheese until smooth. Add apricots and beat to blend well. Preheat oven to 350F (180C). Spread hazelnuts evenly on a rimmed baking sheet and bake about 10 minutes or until lightly toasted. Cool.

Pour nuts onto a paper towel, fold towel around nuts and rub briskly between your palms to remove as much of skins as possible (it's impossible to get them all off). Return nuts to oven and bake 5 minutes longer or until golden. Cool, chop coarsely and add to cheese.

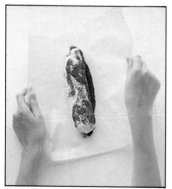

On a sheet of plastic wrap or wax paper, form cheese mixture into an 8-inch-long log. Sprinkle poppy seeds or toasted sesame seeds over cheese log, then roll log so all sides are coated with seeds. Wrap log and refrigerate until firm. To serve, place log on a cheese board and cut in about ⅜-inch-thick slices. Garnish with Italian parsley. Makes about 20 slices.

— BASIL-CHEESE TOASTS —

2 tomatoes
1 (2-oz.) can flat anchovy fillets
10 slices French bread
1 cup shredded Gruyère cheese (4 oz.)
Freshly ground pepper to taste
¼ cup shredded fresh basil leaves
¼ cup olive oil
Basil sprigs

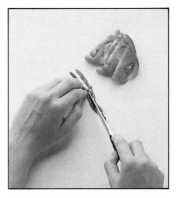

Thinly slice tomatoes. If tomatoes are large, cut each slice in half. Drain anchovies and cut in strips. Set tomatoes and anchovies aside.

Lightly oil a large, shallow baking dish. Preheat oven to 400F (200C). Arrange bread slices in oiled baking dish; sprinkle evenly with cheese. Arrange anchovy strips over cheese; top each bread slice with 1 or 2 tomato slices.

Sprinkle with pepper and some of basil. Drizzle oil over all. Bake 10 to 15 minutes or until bread is crisp and cheese is melted. Sprinkle with remaining basil and garnish with basil sprigs. Serve hot. Makes 10.

- SAGE & ONION PINWHEELS -

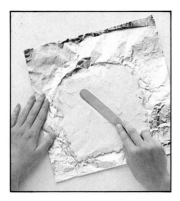

1 (8-oz.) pkg. cream cheese, room temperature
30 fresh, tender sage leaves
3 tablespoons chopped green onions
Freshly ground pepper to taste
Crackers or melba toast, if desired

On a sheet of aluminum foil spread out cream cheese to an 8-inch square.

Lay sage leaves evenly over cheese. Sprinkle with green onions, then sprinkle generously with pepper. Refrigerate for about 20 minutes or until firmer.

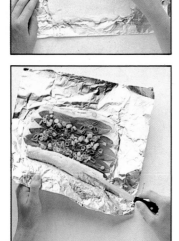

Using foil as a guide, roll up cheese, jelly-roll style, making a compact log. Refrigerate until firm. To serve, cut crosswise in about ⅜-inch-thick slices. Serve plain or on crackers or melba toast. Makes about 20.

VARIATION
If tender sage leaves are unavailable, substitute chopped parsley, tender basil leaves or any other suitable herb.

— CHEESE FILO PASTRIES —

1 lb. feta cheese
3 tablespoons chopped parsley
Freshly ground pepper to taste
3 eggs, beaten
½ cup butter, melted
8 sheets filo pastry

Crumble cheese into a bowl. Add parsley, pepper and eggs. Mix well. Brush two 10″ x 15″ rimmed baking sheets with melted butter. Preheat oven to 400F (200C).

Work with 1 sheet of pastry at a time, keeping remaining pastry covered with damp paper towels or plastic wrap to prevent drying. Cut each sheet in half crosswise, then fold each half-sheet in quarters. Top folded pastry with cheese filling.

Shape pastry around filling like a money bag to enclose. Arrange pastries on buttered baking sheets and brush tops with remaining butter. Bake 20 to 25 minutes or until golden. Serve hot. Makes 16.

— POTTED HERB CHEESE —

2 cups shredded Cheddar cheese (8 oz.)
2 oz. blue-veined cheese
2 tablespoons butter, room temperature
2 tablespoons dry sherry
½ teaspoon Worcestershire sauce
¼ teaspoon prepared hot mustard
1 tablespoon finely chopped mixed fresh herbs
Melba toast or crackers

Place Cheddar cheese in a bowl. Crumble in blue-veined cheese; mix well with a fork. Add butter; beat to blend well.

Gradually beat in sherry, Worcestershire sauce, mustard and herbs.

Pack cheese mixture into a serving bowl, cover and refrigerate at least 1 or 2 days to allow flavor to mingle. Bring to room temperature before serving. Accompany with melba toast or crackers; provide a knife for spreading. Makes about 2½ cups.

——————— TIP ———————

Potted cheese may be mixed in a food processor fitted with a metal blade. Process until the mixture is smooth and thoroughly mixed.

— RICOTTA-CHEESE BALLS —

2 lbs. ricotta cheese (4 cups), well chilled
1 red bell pepper, seeded, finely chopped
¼ cup finely chopped mixed fresh herbs
  (including some green onion, if desired)
¼ cup black sesame seeds or finely chopped
  pistachio nuts
1 teaspoon salt

Line a baking sheet or tray with plastic wrap. Using a small ice-cream scoop or a spoon, shape ricotta cheese into 24 equal balls. Divide ricotta balls into 3 groups of 8 balls each. Roll 1 group in chopped bell pepper.

Roll second group of balls in chopped herbs.

Mix sesame seeds or pistachios and salt, spread on a sheet of wax paper. Roll remaining 8 balls in nut or seed mixture. Arrange all balls on lined baking sheets; cover and refrigerate until ready to serve. To serve, arrange ricotta balls in rows on a platter. Makes 24.

———————— TIP ————————

Black sesame seeds are available in Asian grocery stores.

- MORTADELLA TRIANGLES -

4 oz. ricotta cheese (½ cup)
1 teaspoon prepared horseradish
1 small bunch chives
Salt and pepper to taste
2 or 3 sweet gherkins or dill pickles
3 slices mortadella
Italian parsley
Cherry tomatoes, cut in half

In a bowl, stir together ricotta cheese and horseradish. Snip chives into bowl. Season with salt and pepper.

Cut pickles lengthwise in thin slices. Place 1 mortadella slice on a flat surface; spread with ½ of ricotta mixture, then top evenly with ½ of pickle slices. Add another mortadella slice; press gently. Spread with remaining ricotta mixture; top with remaining pickle slices. Top with remaining mortadella slice.

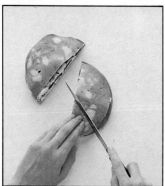

Press gently, then wrap in plastic wrap and refrigerate until firm or up to 24 hours. Using a sharp knife, cut in 8 wedges. Garnish with Italian parsley. Serve on a platter with cherry tomatoes. Makes 8.

— RICOTTA-CHEESE PUFFS

8 oz. ricotta cheese (1 cup)
2 eggs
2 tablespoons all-purpose flour
1 teaspoon salt
3 green onions, chopped
¼ cup chopped parsley
2 teaspoons drained capers, coarsely chopped
Vegetable oil for deep-frying

Place cheese in a bowl and beat until smooth.

Beat in eggs, 1 at a time; then mix in flour, salt, green onions, parsley and capers. If preparing ahead, cover and refrigerate until ready to cook.

To cook, in a large heavy skillet, heat about 2 inches of oil to 350F (180C) or until a 1-inch bread cube turned golden brown in about 65 seconds. Drop rounded teaspoonfuls of ricotta mixture into hot oil, a few at a time. Cook until golden on all sides; drain on paper towels. Serve hot. Makes about 20.

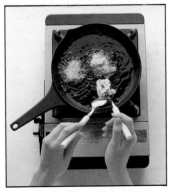

ROQUEFORT SPREAD

4 oz. Roquefort or other blue-veined cheese
4 oz. cream cheese, room temperature
1 tablespoon kirsch or port
½ cup coarsely chopped pecans
Pecan halves
Pear or apple slices or crackers

Crumble Roquefort cheese into a bowl. Bring to room temperature, then beat until smooth.

Add cream cheese and kirsch or port; beat ingredients together until smooth. Stir in chopped pecans. If mixture is very soft, refrigerate until firm enough to handle. Turn out onto a sheet of aluminum foil and shape into 1 large or 2 small rounds.

Arrange pecan halves around cheese ball; refrigerate ball until firm. Serve with pear or apple slices or crackers; provide a knife for spreading. Makes one 8 oz. or two 4 oz. cheese rounds.

ROQUEFORT BISCUITS

1 cup self-raising flour
½ cup firm butter
2 oz. Roquefort or other blue-veined cheese
½ cup shredded Cheddar cheese (2 oz.)
½ cup sesame seeds
Cucumber slices and cherries

Sift flour into a bowl. Using a pastry blender or 2 knives, cut in butter until mixture resembles coarse crumbs. Crumble in Roquefort cheese; sprinkle in Cheddar cheese.

With your fingers, thoroughly mix ingredients to form a dough. Cover and refrigerate. Place sesame seeds in a dry skillet; stir over medium heat until golden. Remove from heat; cool. Preheat oven to 400F (200C). Grease 2 baking sheets. Shape chilled dough into 36 equal balls. Toss each ball in toasted sesame seeds, pressing balls flat to coat well with seeds.

Arrange balls on greased baking sheets and press lightly with a fork. Bake 10 minutes or until golden around edges. Cool on racks and store in an airtight container. To serve, arrange on a plate and garnish with cucumber and cherries. Makes 36.

— DEEP-FRIED CAMEMBERT —

4-oz. Camembert cheese, well chilled
1 egg
½ cup fine dry bread crumbs
¾ cup sesame seeds
Vegetable oil for deep-frying
6 fresh strawberries, if desired

Cut chilled cheese in 6 equal wedges.

In a shallow bowl, beat egg well. On a sheet of wax paper, mix bread crumbs and sesame seeds. Dip each in egg and turn to coat.

Roll cheese in crumb mixture to coat. Place on a plate. If preparing ahead, cover and refrigerate until ready to cook. To cook, in a deep, heavy saucepan, heat about 2 inches of oil to 375F (190C) or until a 1-inch bread cube turns golden brown in about 50 seconds. Add cheese wedges, a few at a time, and cook until golden on all sides. Drain on paper towels. Garnish each wedge with a strawberry, if desired. Serve warm. Makes 6 wedges.

— SPINACH & FETA ROLLS —

2 tablespoons vegetable oil
2 onions, finely chopped
1 (10-oz.) pkg. frozen chopped spinach, thawed
2 teaspoons dried dill weed
4 oz. feta cheese, crumbled
1 egg, beaten
3 tablespoons dairy sour cream
12 sheets filo pastry
½ cup butter, melted

Heat oil in a saucepan over low heat. Add onions and cook, stirring occasionally, until soft but not browned. Meanwhile, drain spinach well, then place in a colander and press out as much water as possible. Stir spinach into onions and cook 2 minutes longer. Stir in dill weed and cheese.

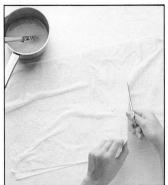

Remove from heat; cool. Mix in egg and sour cream. Cover and refrigerate until cold. Preheat oven to 400F (200C). Work with 2 sheets of pastry at a time, keeping remaining pastry covered with damp paper towels or plastic wrap to prevent drying. Brush 1 sheet with melted butter. Top with another sheet; cut stacked sheets crosswise in 3 strips.

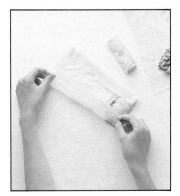

Place a spoonful of filling at 1 end of each strip; tuck in sides and roll up. Brush ends of rolls with melted butter; press lightly to seal. Repeat with remaining sheets of pastry to make 15 more rolls. Place rolls, seam-side down, on baking sheets. Bake about 15 minutes or until golden brown. Serve hot. Makes 18.

– EGG & CHIVE PINWHEELS –

1 (about 1-lb.) loaf unsliced white bread
½ cup butter, room temperature
6 hard-cooked eggs
3 tablespoons mayonnaise
1 teaspoon prepared hot mustard
Salt and pepper to taste
6 tablespoons chopped chives
Italian parsley

Using an electric or serrated knife, trim top of loaf to make it flat. Cut off all crusts, then cut loaf lengthwise in 5 equal slices. Reserve bread trimmings for bread crumbs or other uses, if desired. Spread 1 side of each slice with butter. Set aside.

Shell eggs, cut in chunks and place in a bowl. Add mayonnaise and mustard. Mash ingredients together thoroughly; season with salt and pepper. Spread egg mixture evenly over buttered side of each bread slice, spreading almost to edges. Sprinkle with chives.

Roll up each slice jelly-roll style, starting with short side. Wrap each roll in plastic wrap and refrigerate until ready to serve. To serve, using a serrated or electric knife, cut each roll crosswise in 5 or 6 lengths. Arrange on a platter and garnish with parsley.
Makes 25 to 30.

EGGS TAPENADE

6 hard-cooked eggs
18 ripe olives
5 flat anchovy fillets
1 tablespoon drained capers
1 (3¼-oz.) can tuna, drained
3 tablespoons olive oil
Lemon juice to taste
12 Italian parsley leaves

Shell eggs and cut each in half cross-wise, using a silver or stainless steel knife (carbon steel leaves black marks on egg whites). Remove yolks and place in a food processor fitted with a metal blade. Trim bases of whites so eggs will sit flat. Set whites aside.

Remove pits from 12 olives, then place olives, anchovies, capers and drained tuna and egg yolks in food processor. Process until well blended. With motor running, gradually add oil to make a thick puree. Season with lemon juice. If preparing ahead, cover yolk mixture and refrigerate up to 2 days; place egg whites in a bowl, add cold water to cover and refrigerate up to 2 days. Drain whites, pat dry and fill just before serving.

To fill whites, spoon egg-yolk mixture into cavity of each one. Cut remaining 6 olives in half; place 1 half atop each filled egg half. Garnish with an Italian parsley leaf. Makes 12.

DEVILED EGGS

12 eggs
1 teaspoon prepared hot mustard
6 tablespoons mayonnaise
Few drops of hot-pepper sauce
Pinch of red (cayenne) pepper
2 teaspoons paprika
Rolled anchovy fillets or chopped parsley or
other herbs, to garnish

To boil eggs so yolks are centered, tightly pack them into a saucepan, pointed end down. (You may need to cook eggs in 2 batches.) Pour in enough cold water to cover. Bring to a boil; reduce heat, cover and simmer 10 minutes.

Drain eggs and rinse under cold running water until cool enough to handle. (Quick cooling prevents a black ring forming around yolk.) Shell eggs, then cut each in half lengthwise with a stainless steel or silver knife (carbon steel leaves black marks on egg whites). Place yolks in a bowl and add mustard, mayonnaise, hot-pepper sauce, red pepper and paprika. Mash ingredients together to blend well. Season. Spoon mixture into a pastry bag with a fluted tip.

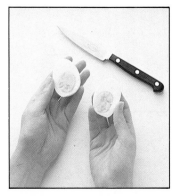

If preparing ahead, refrigerate mixture in pastry bag; place egg whites in a bowl, add cold water to cover and refrigerate. Drain whites, pat dry and fill just before serving. To fill whites, pipe yolk mixture into cavity of each one; garnish. Makes 24.

EGG & SESAME ROLLS

3 eggs
¼ teaspoon salt
1 tablespoon water
2 tablespoons sesame seeds
2 teaspoons dark soy sauce
¼ teaspoon sugar
Salt to taste
½ small onion, finely chopped
1 tablespoon vegetable oil
1 (8-oz.) package frozen chopped spinach,
    thawed
1 thick slice cooked ham, cut in thirds

Lightly beat egg with salt and water; make 3 thin omelets in a 6-inch skillet. Stir sesame seeds in a dry pan over low heat until golden, then grind while hot. Add soy and sugar. Gently cook onion in a oil. Add drained spinach and season to taste. Cool.

Place 1 omelet on rounded side of bamboo placemat. Spread ⅓ of the spinach mixture on 1 end; do not spread to edge. Sprinkle with ⅓ of the sesame seed mixture; place ham strip down center.

Use placemat to help roll omelet; set aside to rest for several minutes wrapped in placemat. Unroll the placemat. Repeat with remaining 2 omelets. Using a sharp knife carefully slice each omelet in four 1¼-inch wide slices. Makes 12.

- EGG-RICOTTA TRIANGLES -

5 eggs
Salt
1 tablespoon water
6 oz. ricotta cheese (¾ cup)
Freshly ground pepper to taste
3 green onions, chopped
¼ cup chopped parsley
2 teaspoons drained capers, chopped
½ red bell pepper, seeded, cut in strips

In a bowl beat 3 eggs, about ⅛ teaspoon salt and water until blended. Heat 6-inch skillet over medium heat and grease lightly. Make 3 separate omelets with the egg mixture.

In another bowl, beat together ricotta cheese, remaining 2 eggs, 1 teaspoon salt, pepper, green onions, parsley and capers. Place 1 omelet on a heatproof plate small enough to fit comfortably in a steaming basket. Spread omelet ⅓ of cheese mixture. Top with ⅓ of bell-pepper strips. Repeat with remaining omelets, cheese mixtures and bell-pepper strips.

Place plate in steaming basket. Cover and steam over boiling water 15 minutes; make sure steam can circulate all around plates. Serve warm or cold. If serving warm, cool slightly; then cut into about 8 triangles. If serving cold, cool, then refrigerate until cold. Cut into wedges. Makes about 8.

— EGG & CAVIAR SPREAD —

4 eggs
¼ cup butter
Salt and freshly ground pepper to taste
½ cup dairy sour cream
4 green onions or ½ small white onion, finely
   chopped
3 tablespoons black caviar
Crackers

Place eggs in a saucepan and pour in enough cold water to cover. Bring to a boil; then reduce heat, cover and simmer 10 minutes. Drain eggs and rinse under cold running water until cool enough to handle. Shell eggs, cut in chunks and place in a bowl.

Melt butter in a small saucepan. Mash eggs thoroughly; pour hot melted butter over warm mashed eggs. Season with salt and pepper. Pack egg mixture into a serving dish; cover and refrigerate up to 24 hours.

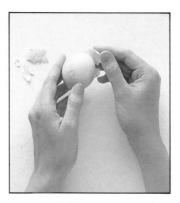

Just before serving, in a small bowl, stir together sour cream and green onion or white onion. Spread over egg mixture. Top with caviar. If desired, garnish with lemon or lime slices or wedges and parsley sprigs. Serve with crackers; provide a small knife for spreading. Makes 1½ to 2 cups.

QUICK DIPS

CREAM CORN DIP

1 (10-oz.) jar corn relish
1¼ cups dairy sour cream
Crackers or corn ships

Stir together corn relish and sour cream, then spoon into a serving bowl. Serve with crackers or corn chips for dipping. Makes about 1½ cups.

CAVIAR DIP

1¼ cups dairy sour cream
1 tablespoon finely chopped onion
1 (2-oz.) jar red caviar
Italian parsley
Crackers or crisp raw vegetables

Stir together sour cream, onion and ½ of caviar, then spoon into a serving bowl. Swirl in remaining caviar. Garnish and serve with crackers or vegetables for dipping. Makes about 1¼ cups.

ANCHOVY DIP

1 (2-oz.) can flat anchovy fillets, drained
1¼ cups dairy sour cream
3 tablespoons chopped dill pickle
2 teaspoons drained capers
Crackers

Coarsely chop anchovies, then mash well. Stir together sour cream, anchovies and pickle, then spoon into a serving bowl. Garnish with capers. Serve with crackers for dipping. Makes about 1½ cups.

AIOLI & CRUDITÉS

4 garlic cloves
About ½ teaspoon salt
2 egg yolks
1 cup olive oil
Juice of ½ lemon
Crisp raw vegetables, such as carrot sticks,
celery sticks, small whole radishes,
cauliflowerets, edible-pod peas, cucumber
sticks, blanched fresh asparagus spears and
green onions.

Press garlic through a garlic press into a bowl. Add ½ teaspoon salt and egg yolks; beat well with a whisk. Add 1 or 2 drops oil and whisk well.

Gradually add about 2 more table-spoons oil, whisking constantly. Then, still whisking constantly, add remaining oil in a thin stream. If mixture becomes too thick, add a little hot water. When all oil has been added, whisk in lemon juice and season with additional salt, if needed. Cover aioli and refrigerate until ready to use.

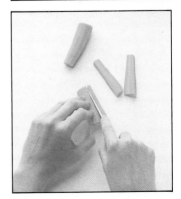

Prepare the uncooked vegetables; cut the carrots in 3-inch sticks, slice the cucumber and trim the celery, radishes, cauliflowers and green onions. To serve, spoon aioli into a serving bowl and place in center of a large platter. Arrange vegetables around aioli; dip vegetables in aioli before eating. Makes about 1 cup aioli.

BAGNA CAUDA

Crisp raw vegetables, such as 2 or 3 carrots,
edible-pod peas and ½ cauliflower
1 (2-oz.) can flat anchovy fillets, drained
½ cup butter
½ cup olive oil or vegetable oil
4 garlic cloves, crushed
½ pint whipping cream (1 cup)
Crusty bread, sliced

Cut carrots in 4-inch pieces, then cut in thin strips. Separate cauliflower into flowerets; trim and rinse the edible-pod peas. Mash the anchovies.

Melt butter in oil in a saucepan; stir in mashed anchovies and garlic. Bring to a gentle boil, stirring constantly; then reduce heat and simmer 5 minutes. Stir in cream. Heat, stirring, about 5 minutes or until sauce is thickened; do not boil.

To serve, pour hot anchovy sauce into a warmed bowl or a chafing dish. Arrange vegetables and a basket of bread around sauce. Let guests spear vegetables with wooden skewers, then dip in sauce and eat with a slice of bread to catch the drips. Makes about 2 cups sauce.

── MEXICAN BEAN DIP ──

1 (15-oz.) can red kidney beans
2 tablespoons vegetable oil
¾ cup shredded Cheddar cheese (3 oz.)
Salt to taste
1 teaspoon chili powder
1 tablespoon chopped green bell pepper
Deep-fried shrimp chips, see below

Drain beans, reserving liquid.

Heat oil in a medium skillet; add drained beans and heat through, mashing with a potato masher or fork. Add 3 tablespoons reserved bean liquid and stir well. Remove from heat; cool. Stir in cheese, salt and chili powder. Heat through over low heat. If mixture is too thick, stir in more reserved bean liquid until mixture has a good consistency for scooping with chips. Stir in bell pepper. Serve dip hot, with corn or deep-fried shrimp chips. Makes about 1½ cups.

DEEP FRIED SHRIMP CHIPS
Shrimp chips are available from Asian grocery stores. Drop a few at a time into deep hot oil and when they come to the surface, remove at once; chips take only a few seconds to cook. Drain on paper towels; store in an airtight container until ready to serve.

PEANUT SAUCE

2 garlic cloves
2 tablespoons dark soy sauce
¼ cup smooth peanut butter
1 tablespoon sugar
1 cup water
2 small, fresh, red hot chilies, seeded
Crisp raw vegetables, such as carrots, celery, cucumbers, green beans, small whole radishes, cauliflowerets (blanched, if desired) and edible-pod peas

Crush garlic into a small saucepan with the soy sauce, peanut butter, sugar and water.

Cut the chillies in small slivers and add to the saucepan. Bring to a simmer; then simmer 5 minutes, stirring constantly. If sauce is very thin, simmer until slightly thickened. Remove from heat; cool to room temperature before serving. If sauce solidifies upon cooling, thin it with a little hot water.

Prepare vegetables; cut carrots, celery and cucumber into 2-inch pieces, then cut in thin strips. To serve, pour sauce into a serving bowl and place in center of a platter. Arrange vegetables of your choice around sauce. Dip vegetables in sauce before eating. Makes about ¼ cup sauce.

GUACAMOLE

3 ripe avocados
2 tablespoons lemon juice
1 garlic clove, crushed
1 small onion, finely chopped
Few drops of hot-pepper sauce
Salt to taste
4 bacon slices
Corn chips

Cut 2 avocados in half; remove pits and scoop flesh into a food processor fitted with a metal blade.

Add lemon juice, garlic, onion and hot-pepper sauce. Process until smooth. Season with salt and more hot-pepper sauce, if desired. If preparing ahead, cover airtight and refrigerate up to 2 hours. If kept longer, the guacamole will begin to darken. Placing the avocado pits in the guacamole will help prevent browning; remove them before serving.

To serve, in a skillet, cook bacon until crisp. Drain, cool and crumble. Stir into guacamole. Pit, peel and dice remaining avocado and stir into guacamole. Serve with corn chips. Serves 6 to 8.

HUMMUS BI TAHINI

½ cup plus 1 tablespoon dried garbanzo beans
About 2 teaspoons salt
4 garlic cloves
½ cup tahini
Lemon juice to taste
About 1 tablespoon olive oil
Paprika and Italian parsley sprigs
Pocket bread, cut in wedges

Rinse and sort beans, then soak overnight in cold water to cover.

Drain and place in a saucepan. Pour in enough cold water to cover; stir in 2 teaspoons salt. Bring to a boil; reduce heat, cover and simmer 2 hours or until beans are very tender. Drain, reserving cooking liquid. Place drained beans in a food processor fitted with a metal blade. Process to make a smooth paste, adding a little reserved cooking liquid as needed. Add garlic, tahini and lemon juice. Process until blended. Add salt.

Turn hummus into a serving bowl, smooth surface and drizzle with enough oil to make a thin layer (this prevents drying). Garnish with paprika and 1 or 2 Italian parsley sprigs. Serve with pocket-bread wedges. Serves 12 to 15.

VARIATION:
If desired, split pocket bread, tear in pieces and bake in a 300F (150C) oven 10 to 15 minutes or until crisp.

MINTED SAMBAL DIP

4 green onions
1¼ cups dairy sour cream
1 teaspoon finely grated fresh gingerroot
1 tablespoon lemon juice
1 tablespoon curry powder
½ cup chopped fresh mint
1 garlic clove
1 teaspoon salt
Celery and other crisp vegetables

With a sharp knife, finely chop green onion, including tops. In a large bowl, mix together chopped green onion, sour cream, grated ginger root, lemon juice, curry powder and chopped mint.

Use the tip of a strong knife to crush the garlic in salt until it forms a pulp; add to dairy sour cream mixture. If mixture is thin, whip until thickened and stir well. Cover and refrigerate at least 24 hours.

To serve, prepare vegetables for crudités; cut celery sticks in 4-inch thin strips. Place the dip in the center of a platter and surround with the vegetables for dipping. Serves 4.

SKEWERED BITES

PROSCIUTTO & MELON

1 small cantaloupe
½ lb. very thinly sliced prosciutto

Peel melon, cut in half and scoop out seeds. Cut flesh in cubes. To make each skewer, gather up a slice of prosciutto and skewer onto a melon cube with a wooden pick. Refrigerate until chilled, then serve. Makes about 48.

AVOCADO & SHRIMP

1 ripe avocado
1 lb. cooked large or jumbo shrimp, shelled,
** deveined**
Lemon juice

Halve and pit avocado. Scoop flesh from each half with a melon-ball cutter; or peel halves, then cut in cubes. Skewer 1 shrimp and 1 avocado piece on each wooden pick. Sprinkle with lemon juice and serve immediately. Makes about 18.

SMOKED–BEEF ROLLS

2 tablespoons dairy sour cream
1 teaspoon prepared horseradish
¼ lb. thinly sliced smoked beef

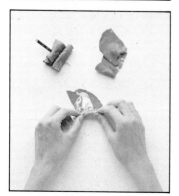

Stir together sour cream and horseradish. Spread mixture on beef slices; roll up, slice and cut in 1-inch pieces. Skewer 2 or 3 pieces on each wooden pick. Makes 8 to 10.

— DEVILED MIXED NUTS —

¾ cup whole almonds
1 cup raw cashews
1 cup pecan halves
3 tablespoons butter
2 garlic cloves, crushed
1 teaspoon Worcestershire sauce
2 teaspoons curry powder
Pinch of red cayenne pepper

To blanch almonds, pour boiling water over nuts in a heatproof bowl, leave a few minutes, then lift out. The nuts will easily slip out of the skins.

Preheat oven to 350F (180C). Place almonds, cashews and pecans in a bowl. Melt butter in a saucepan and stir in garlic, Worcestershire sauce, curry powder and red pepper. Drizzle butter mixture evenly over nuts and toss to coat evenly.

Spread nuts in a baking dish; bake 15 to 20 minutes, or until golden, stirring every 5 minutes to toast evenly. Remove from oven and cool. Store in an airtight container until ready to serve. Makes about 3 cups.

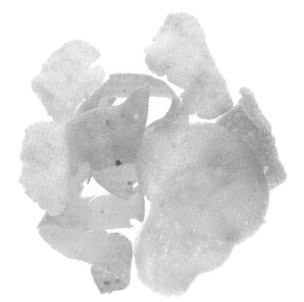

FRIED TREATS

MELINJO NUTS

These are the kernels of an Indonesian nut, dried and flattened out into thin wafers. They're sold in Asian grocery stores. To cook melinjo nuts, deep-fry the wafers in hot oil (350F/180C), a few at a time, until they puff. Avoid browning the wafers; this gives them a bitter taste. Drain on paper towels and sprinkle with salt before serving.

SHRIMP CHIPS

Available in Asian grocery stores and well-stocked supermarkets, shrimp chips are sold in dried form and must be deep-fried before eating. They come in a variety of colors, but the plain (uncolored) ones usually have a better flavor. To cook the chips, deep-fry them in hot oil (350F/180C) a few at a time, until they puff and turn crisp (this takes only a few seconds). Drain on paper towels. If prepared ahead, store cooled chips in airtight containers up to 2 days.

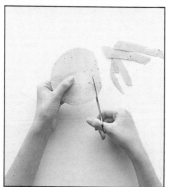

POPPADAM STRIPS

With scissors, cut poppadams in strips about ½ inch wide. Deep-fry strips in hot oil (350F/180C), a few at a time, until golden and crisp. Drain on paper towels and serve with drinks. If desired, dust the strips with paprika mixed with a pinch of red (cayenne) pepper while still hot.

— SPICED CRACKED OLIVES —

2 lbs. large green olives, drained
2-3 small, whole, dried red hot chilies
4 garlic cloves
3 dill sprigs
3 thyme sprigs
3 oregano sprigs
2 teaspoons fennel seeds
Olive oil

Make a lengthwise cut in each olive, cutting in as far as the pit. (This allows flavors from the marinade to penetrate.)

Place olives, chilies, garlic, dill sprigs, thyme sprigs, oregano sprigs and fennel seeds in a large jar. Pour in enough oil to cover. Cover jar tightly; refrigerate at least several days before serving. Drain; serve as an appetizer with drinks or use in salads. You may reserve oil and add more olives to it; or use oil for cooking or in salad dressings. Makes about 1¾ lb.

CALAMATTA OLIVES WITH GARLIC
Calamatta olives
Garlic cloves
Small, whole, dried red hot chilies, if desired
Olive oil (or half olive oil, half vegetable oil)

In a jar, combine olives and garlic cloves. Add a few chilies for added bite, if desired. Pour in enough oil to cover olives. Cover jar tightly and refrigerate at least several days before serving. Drain; serve with drinks.

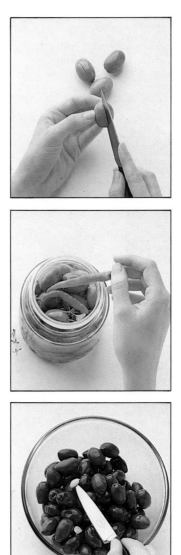

— PICKLED VEGETABLES —

½ lb. cauliflower
½ lb. slender carrots
1 red bell pepper
1 cup white wine vinegar
¼ cup sugar
1 teaspoon salt
1 teaspoon mustard seeds
1 teaspoon black peppercorns
¼ lb. edible-pod peas

Separate cauliflower into flowerets. Peel carrots and cut in about 4-inch lengths. Seed bell pepper and cut lengthwise in strips.

Drop cauliflower, carrots and bell pepper into a saucepan full of boiling water. Return to a full boil; then drain vegetables, rinse under cold running water and drain again. Set aside.

In a large bowl, combine vinegar, sugar, salt, mustard seeds and peppercorns. Stir until sugar is dissolved. Stir in cauliflower, carrots and bell pepper. Cover and refrigerate 2 days, stirring occasionally so vegetables will absorb flavor evenly. Two hours before serving, remove ends and strings from peas; stir into vegetable mixture. Cover and refrigerate until cold. Serve vegetables cold, with a dipping sauce. Serves 6 to 8.

EGG & NORI ROLLS

3 sheets nori (dried laver seaweed)
3 eggs
Pinch of salt
1 tablespoon cold water

Toast each sheet of nori until crisp by running it quickly back and forth over a gas flame or above an electric element set on medium heat. Be careful not to burn nori. Set toasted nori aside.

In a bowl, beat together eggs, salt and water. Heat a skillet on a medium heat; grease lightly. Set 1 teaspoon egg mixture aside. Use the remaining egg mixture to make 4 thin omelets. Trim nori sheets to same size as omelets.

Place omelet, uncooked-side up, on a bamboo mat. Top with 1 sheet nori. Continue stacking omelets and nori sheets until all are used. Roll up omelet-nori stack in mat to make a tight, compact cylinder; seal seam with reserved egg mixture. Let stand until cold. Remove bamboo mat; cut roll in chunks. Makes about 12.

TIP

Nori is dried laver seaweed. The greenish-black sheets are sold in Asian grocery stores and some well-stocked supermarkets.

STUFFED FRUITS

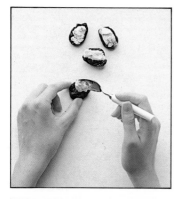

PRUNES WITH WALNUT FILLING

2 oz. cream cheese, room temperature
1 tablespoon chopped walnuts
12 pitted prunes
Walnut halves to garnish

In a small bowl, beat cream cheese
and walnuts until blended. Stuff mixture into prunes and garnish. Refrigerate before serving. Makes 12.

FIGS WITH CAMEMBERT

½ lb. dried figs
3 tablespoons port
1 (4 oz.) whole Camembert cheese

In a bowl, combine figs and port.
Cover and let soak several hours.
Then cut a slit in each fig; gently
hollow inside of fig with your finger.
Cut cheese in as many pieces as you
have figs; fill each fig with a piece of
cheese. Makes about 15.

FRESH DATES WITH GINGER

½ lb. fresh or dried dates
4 oz. cream cheese, room temperature
1 tablespoon chopped crystallized ginger
1 teaspoon grated lemon peel

Remove pits from dates. In a small
bowl, beat cream cheese, ginger and
lemon peel until blended. Stuff mixture into dates. Makes about 15.

POOR-MAN'S CAVIAR

2 eggplants
Salt
Freshly ground pepper to taste
¼ cup olive oil
1 garlic clove, crushed
2 flat anchovy fillets, if desired
2 tablespoons distilled white vinegar
1 tablespoon lemon juice
Lemon slices, fresh fennel and parsley sprigs

Halve eggplants. Score cut sides deeply in a diamond pattern and sprinkle flesh liberally with salt. Place eggplant halves, cut-side down, in a larger, shallow dish. Let stand 1 to 2 hours. Preheat oven to 350F (180C).

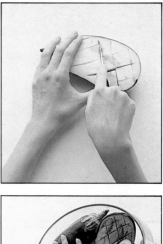

Drain all juices from eggplants, then rinse under cold running water. Drain well; pat dry. Arrange on a rimmed baking sheet, cut-side up; sprinkle with pepper and drizzle with 2 tablespoons oil. Bake 1 hour or until eggplant is very soft when pierced with a skewer.

Cool eggplant slightly, then scoop flesh into a food processor fitted with a metal blade. Add garlic and anchovies, if desired; process until smooth. With motor running, gradually add remaining 2 tablespoons oil; drop-by-drop at first, increasing to a thin stream. Continue to process until mixture is thick. Stir in vinegar and lemon juice. Garnish. Makes 8 to 10 servings.

—MARINATED ARTICHOKES—

1 (14 oz) can artichoke hearts packed in water, drained
6 tablespoons olive oil or vegetable oil
Freshly ground pepper to taste
3 tablespoons chopped mixed fresh herbs, such as parsley, basil and oregano
Lemon juice and salt to taste
Toast rounds, if desired

Rinse artichoke hearts well in cold water. Drain, pat dry and cut lengthwise in halves or quarters.

Place in a bowl and add oil, pepper and herbs. Mix well. Cover and refrigerate at least 4 hours or until ready to serve. For longer storage, place artichokes in a jar, making sure they are covered with oil; cover tightly and refrigerate up to 2 weeks. To serve, bring to room temperature. Stir well; season with lemon juice and salt. Offer wooden picks for picking up artichoke; or serve artichokes on toast rounds. Provide small napkins. If desired, add artichokes to salads. Makes about 1¼ cups.

VARIATIONS
For added bite, mix a few slivers of fresh, red hot chili into the marinade. If you're a garlic lover, add a crushed garlic clove.

——— ASPARAGUS ROLLS ———

25 fresh or canned asparagus spears
1 cup butter
4 egg yolks
1 tablespoon chopped fresh mint
Lemon juice to taste
25 thin slices firm-textured white bread

If using fresh asparagus, snap off and discard tough stalk ends. Wash stalks in cold water, then cook about 8 minutes in boiling water. Drain, rinse under cold running water and drain again. If using canned asparagus, drain well. Set asparagus aside.

To make sauce, melt butter in a small saucepan and keep very hot. Process egg yolks in a food processor fitted with a metal blade until frothy. With motor running, gradually add hot melted butter in a thin stream; process until blended. Transfer to a bowl; cover and refrigerate until mixture is thickened. Stir in mint and lemon juice.

Preheat broiler. Trim crusts from bread slices, then spread bread with sauce. Cut each asparagus spear in half; place 2 halves on each bread slice. Bring 2 opposite corners to center of each slice; fasten with a wooden pick. Dot with more sauce. Arrange asparagus rolls on a baking sheet; broil until crisp and golden. Makes 25.

CRISP SPLIT PEAS

1 cup yellow split peas
2 teaspoons baking soda
Vegetable oil for deep-frying
½ teaspoon chili powder
½ teaspoon ground coriander
Pinch of ground cinnamon
Pinch of ground cloves
1 teaspoon salt

Rinse and sort peas, then place in a large bowl and add enough cold water to cover. Stir in baking soda. Let soak overnight.

Drain peas, rinse several times in cold water and drain thoroughly. Let stand at least 30 minutes, then spread out on paper towels and let dry thoroughly. In a deep, heavy saucepan, heat about 2 inches of oil to 350F (180C) or until a 1-inch bread cube turns golden brown in about 65 seconds. Add peas, a portion at a time, and cook until golden. (Be careful when cooking peas; even when completely dry, they often cause oil to bubble to top of pan.) Remove peas from hot oil with a slotted spoon and drain on paper towels.

Turn cooked peas into a small bowl. Sprinkle with chili powder, coriander, cinnamon, cloves and salt; mix to coat peas with spice mixture. Cool completely; store in an airtight container until ready to serve. Makes about 1¾ cups.

— CUCUMBER SANDWICHES —

2 cucumbers
1 tablespoon salt
24 thin slices firm-textured white or
**   wholewheat bread**
½ cup butter, room temperature
Freshly ground pepper to taste
3 tablespoons dairy sour cream
1 bunch chives, chopped

Thinly slice cucumbers. (If using a tough-skinned variety, peel and seed before slicing.) Arrange cucumber slices in a single layer on a flat platter or in a large rimmed baking dish. Sprinkle with salt. Cover cucumber slices with a plate (or plates); top plate with a weight, such as canned goods. Let stand several hours.

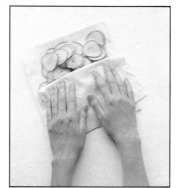

Drain all juices from cucumber slices; then rinse under cold running water to remove excess salt. Drain well between several layers of paper towels. Cover and refrigerate until ready to use.

Trim crusts from bread slices; spread 1 side of each slice with butter. Top buttered side of 12 slices with cucumber slices; spinkle with pepper. Cover with remaining bread slices, buttered-side down. Cut each sandwich diagonally in quarters. Spread sour cream on 1 cut side of each triangle, then dip in chives. Arrange on a platter and serve. Makes 48.

CUCUMBER & SALMON ROLLS

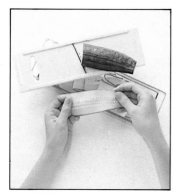

1 English cucumber
10 slices smoked salmon
Prepared horseradish
Pickled ginger, cut in thin strips

Trim ends from cucumber, then cut cucumber in 5-inch lengths. Using a mandolin, Japanese vegetable slicer or vegetable peeler, cut cucumber lengthwise in very thin slices. Cut salmon slices in 3-inch-long strips of the same width as cucumber slices.

Thinly spread each cucumber slice with horseradish, then top with a salmon strip. Place a few pickled ginger strips on 1 end of each cucumber slice.

Roll up cucumber slices, starting with pickled-ginger end. Secure rolls closed by dabbing "seam" with a little horseradish and pressing lightly. Place rolls on a platter with ginger facing up; serve immediately. Makes 20.

――――――――――― TIP ―――――――

Red pickled ginger is sold in Asian grocery stores and some well-stocked supermarkets.

– MARINATED MUSHROOMS –

1 lb. small fresh mushrooms
1 cup water
2 teaspoons salt
½ cup distilled white vinegar
1 bay leaf
Few thyme sprigs
1 garlic clove
2 tablespoons olive oil
Sliced green onion or mild red onion, if
desired.
Finely chopped parsley
Peel of 1 lemon, cut in thin strips

Trim mushroom stems. Wipe mushrooms with a cloth dipped in cold acidulated water (1½ teaspoons lemon juice or distilled white vinegar to 2 cups water). Place mushrooms in a heatproof bowl.

In a saucepan, combine 1 cup water, salt, vinegar, bay leaf, thyme sprigs, garlic and oil. Bring to a boil; pour over mushrooms. Cool, then cover and refrigerate at least 12 hours or up to 3 days.

To serve, drain mushrooms and place in a serving bowl. Discard bay leaf, thyme and garlic. If desired, gently mix in sliced onion. Sprinkle with parsley and lemon peel. If desired, offer wooden picks for picking up mushrooms; provide small napkins. Makes about 3 cups.

MUSHROOM PASTIES

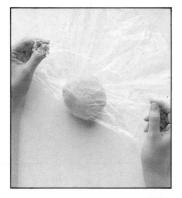

1 cup plus 1 tablespoon all-purpose flour
6 tablespoons firm butter
1 to 2 tablespoons cold water
3 green onions, chopped
½ lb. small fresh mushrooms, chopped
¼ teaspoon dry mustard
1 tablespoon dry sherry
2 tablespoons milk
8 pitted ripe olives, sliced
Salt and pepper to taste
1 egg, beaten

Sift 1 cup flour into a bowl. Using a pastry blender or 2 knives, cut in 4 tablespoons butter until mixture resembles coarse crumbs. Sprinkle in cold water, stirring with a fork until dough holds together. Gather into a ball; wrap and chill 30 minutes.

Melt remaining 2 tablespoons butter in a large skillet. Add green onions and cook, stirring, until soft but not browned. Add mushrooms and cook, stirring, until all liquid has evaporated. Stir in remaining 1 tablespoon flour; then stir in mustard, sherry and milk. Bring to a boil, stirring. Stir in olives and season. Remove from heat. Chill.

Preheat oven to 400F (200C). Grease 2 baking sheets. On a floured board, roll out pastry thinly and cut into 3-inch rounds. Place a teaspoonful of filling in center of each round. Brush up edges and join in center; pinch. Brush tops with egg. Bake 15 to 20 minutes. Makes 10.

AVOCADO MOUSSE

2 tablespoons unflavored gelatin
1 cup cold water
2 avocados
2 tablespoons lemon juice
2 teaspoons salt
1 tablespoon whipping cream
Avocado slices and chopped red pepper
Crackers or melba toast

In a small saucepan, soften gelatin in cold water. Then place over low heat and stir until gelatin is dissolved. Remove from heat; set aside. Halve and pit 2 avocados. Scoop flesh into a food processor fitted with a metal blade. Add lemon juice, salt and gelatin. Process. Add cream and blend.

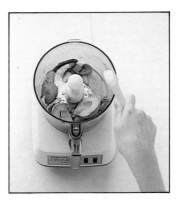

Rinse individual molds with cold water; pour in avocado. Refrigerate.

To serve, dip each mold up to rim in hot water. Invert onto a platter; lift off molds, easing out with a knife. Garnish with avocado slices and bell pepper. Serve with crackers or melba toast. Makes 4 to 6 servings.

To make mousse in a loaf pan, first make this glaze: in a small saucepan, soften 1 tablespoon unflavored gelatin in 1 cup cold homemade or canned chicken stock. Then place over low heat and stir until gelatin is dissolved. Rinse loaf pan with cold water. Pour ½ of gelatin mixture into loaf pan and refrigerate until set. Garnish; evenly pour on remaining glaze and refrigerate until set. Pour in Avocado Mousse. Chill until set; unmold.

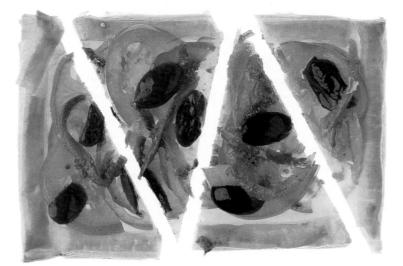

PISSALADIÈRE

3 sheets (1½ x 17½ oz. pkg.) frozen puff pastry, thawed
3 or 4 tomatoes
Freshly ground pepper to taste
6 to 8 calamatta olives
1 (2 oz.) can flat anchovy fillets, drained
1 egg, beaten
Chopped fresh basil, if desired

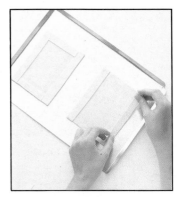

Unfold pastry sheets. Cut each sheet of pastry into two 5" x 6" rectangles. Arrange rectangles on ungreased baking sheets. Cut pastry trimmings in ½-inch wide strips and place along edges of pastry rectangles to form borders.

Prick centers of pastry rectangles with a fork.

Preheat oven to 400F (200C). Halve tomatoes, then thinly slice crosswise. Arrange tomatoes in even rows on pastries, slightly overlapping slices. Sprinkle generously with pepper. Cut olive flesh away from pits; arrange olives and anchovies over tomatoes. Brush borders of pastries with egg. Bake 10–15 minutes or until pastry is golden. Cut each pastry in 4 triangles and sprinkle with basil, if desired. Serve warm. Makes 24 pieces.

MINI-PIZZAS

1 (¼-oz.) pkg. active dry yeast
1 teaspoon sugar
1 cup warm water (110F, 45C)
2½ cups all-purpose flour
½ teaspoon salt
2 tablespoons vegetable oil
2 onions, chopped
2 garlic cloves, crushed
4 to 6 tomatoes, peeled, sliced
2 teaspoons tomato paste
Salt and pepper to taste
¼ lb. sliced pepperoni, cut in small pieces
4 oz. mozzarella cheese, cut in cubes
20 pitted ripe olives

Dissolve yeast and sugar with ½ cup warm water. Let stand until bubbly. Stir together flour and ½ teaspoon salt. Mix in yeast mixture and remaining ½ cup warm water. Knead on a well-floured board at least 5 minutes or until smooth and elastic. Place dough in greased bowl and turn.

Cover and let rise in a warm place about 1 hour or until doubled in bulk. Heat oil in a large skillet. Add onions and garlic; cook, stirring, 2 minutes. Stir in tomatoes and simmer, uncovered, 20 minutes. Add tomato paste and season.

Preheat oven to 400F (200C). Punch down dough, turn out onto a floured board and knead lightly. Roll out to ½-inch thick and cut into 3-inch rounds. Arrange on greased baking sheets. Top with tomato sauce, pepperoni, cheese and olives. Bake 20 to 30 minutes. Makes 12.

SUSHI ROLLED IN SEAWEED

1 Sushi Rice recipe, page 22
6 dried Chinese mushrooms
2 tablespoons soy sauce
2 teaspoons sugar
1 cucumber
2 carrots
6 sheets nori (dried laver seaweed)

Prepare Sushi Rice; set aside. Place mushrooms in a bowl, pour in enough boiling water to cover and let soak 20 minutes. Drain. Cut off and discard stems; thinly slice caps. In a saucepan, combine sliced caps, soy sauce and sugar. Cook, stirring often, until liquid has evaporated. Remove from heat. Peel cucumber and carrots and cut lengthwise in thin strips. Set all vegetables aside. Toast nori until crisp by drawing it quickly back and forth over a gas flame or above an electric element set on medium. Be careful not to burn nori. Place 1 sheet of nori on a bamboo mat; spread ⅙ of sushi rice over nori, covering ⅔ of surface of seaweed.

Arrange 1/6 of cucumber and carrot strips in a line down rice. Top evenly with 1/6 of mushrooms.

Roll nori around rice and vegetables, using mat to help you and pressing firmly to form a neat cylinder. Let stand 10 minutes. Remove bamboo mat; cut roll crosswise in 6 pieces. Repeat with remaining nori, rice and vegetables. Serve cold. Makes 36.

— GINGERED FRUIT KEBABS —

1 cantaloupe or honeydew melon (or some of
  each)
About 1 pint fresh strawberries
1¼ cups dairy sour cream or plain yogurt
1 tablespoon honey
1 tablespoon chopped crystallized ginger
1 tablespoon chopped fresh mint
Mint sprigs, if desired

Peel melon; cut in half, scoop out
seeds and cut flesh in bite-size pieces.
Wash and hull strawberries; halve.

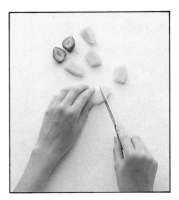

Thread fruit on about 20 bamboo
skewers, alternating melon chunks
and berries. If preparing ahead,
arrange skewered fruits in a container, cover and refrigerate up to 4
hours.

In a small bowl, stir together, sour
cream or yogurt, honey, ginger and
chopped mint. Cover and refrigerate
until ready to serve, then transfer to a
serving bowl. Place bowl in center of
a platter; surround with fruit kebabs.
If desired, garnish with mint sprigs.
Dip fruit in sour-cream sauce before
eating. Makes about 20.

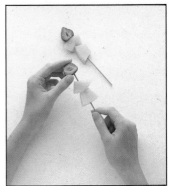

--------------------- TIP ---------------------

In place of melon and strawberries, you may use any
suitable fruit in season – pineapple, apples, pears, or
citrus fruit, for example.

LAMB TRIANGLES

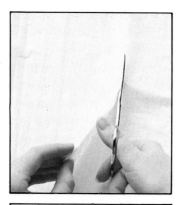

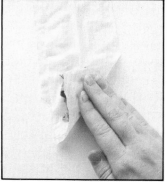

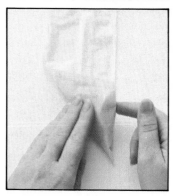

1 tablespoon vegetable oil
1 garlic clove, crushed
1 teaspoon grated fresh gingerroot
1 onion, finely chopped
1 tablespoon curry powder
1 tablespoon white-wine vinegar
½ lb. ground cooked lamb
½ cup water
2 tablespoons chopped fresh mint
Salt to taste
1 egg, beaten
3 sheets filo pastry
½ cup butter, melted

Heat oil in a large skillet over low heat. Add garlic, gingerroot and onion; cook for 1 minute, stirring. Add curry powder and cook for 1 more minute, stirring. Stir in vinegar, ground lamb and water, then simmer for 5 minutes. Add mint and salt. Remove from heat. Mix in egg; cool. Preheat oven to 400F (200C); lightly grease baking sheets. Cut pastry in 2-inch strips.

Work with 1 double strip of pastry at a time, keeping remaining pastry covered with a damp paper towel or plastic wrap to prevent drying. Brush 1 strip with melted butter. Place a spoonful of lamb in one corner and fold to form a triangle.

Continue folding, keeping the shape, until whole strip is used; press to seal and brush top with melted butter. Repeat with remaining pastry. Place on baking sheets; bake 20 minutes. Serve warm. Makes 30 to 35.

DOLMADES

1 (8-oz.) jar grape leaves
2 tablespoons olive oil
1 onion, finely chopped
2 cups cooked long-grain white rice
Salt and pepper to taste
2 tablespoons chopped fresh mint
1 cup toasted pine nuts
Fresh mint sprigs if desired

Drain grape leaves and rinse well; then soak in cold water to cover to remove brine, separating leaves carefully. Drain and set aside.

Heat oil in a medium skillet. Add onion and cook, stirring, until tender. Remove from heat and stir in rice, salt, pepper, mint and ½ cup toasted pine nuts. Place about 2 teaspoons filling on each leaf; roll up leaf, tucking in edges.

Arrange filled leaves close together in large skillet. If necessary, make more than 1 layer; separate layers with leftover grape leaves. Pour in enough hot water to barely cover filled leaves. Place a heatproof plate directly on top of leaves; place a weight (such as canned goods) on top of plate. Cover and simmer 30 minutes. Remove from heat; cool. Cover and refrigerate until cold. Garnish with ½ cup toasted pine nuts or fresh mint sprigs, if desired. Makes about 45.

Clockwise from top: Spicy Pork Rolls, page 45; Almond-Cheese
Balls, page 72; Chicken Satay, page 55

Avocado Mousse, page 115

Clockwise from top: Chinese Dumplings, page 44; Chicken & Leek
Rolls, page 58, Spring Rolls, page 43

Sushi With Shrimp, page 22; Sushi Rolled In Seaweed, page 118

Clockwise from top: Cucumber & Salmon Rolls, page 112; Sage & Onion Pinwheels, page 76; Eggs Tapenade, page 87; Spiced Cracked Olives, page 103

Salmon & Avocado Mousse, page 28

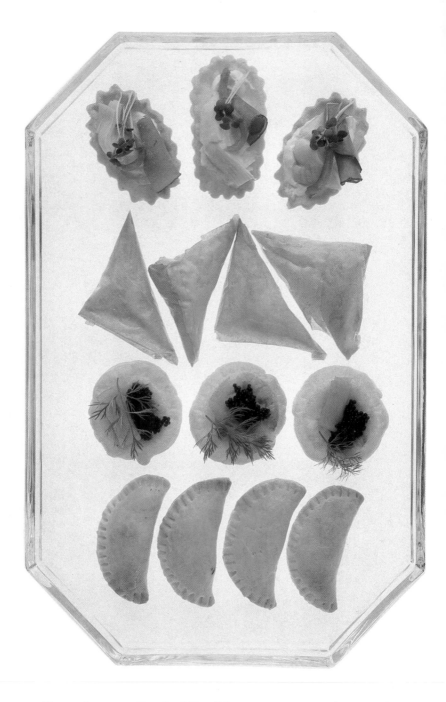

Top to bottom: Smoked Beef Tarts, page 61; Lamb Triangles,
page 120; Smoked-Salmon Quiches, page 30; Ham Crescents, page 39

Caviar Molds, page 14

INDEX